Cash Rules:

Reminiscences
of a Day Trader

David Hale

Cash Rules:

Reminiscences of a Day Trader

© David Hale, 2023

https://www.david-hale.com/

Cover artwork by Dymitrij Gold

Editing and formatting: Tim Clayton

All rights reserved. No part of this publication may be reproduced, stored in a retrieval system, or transmitted, in any form or by any means without prior written permission of the author, nor be otherwise circulated in any form of binding or cover other than that in which it is published and without a similar condition being imposed on the subsequent purchaser.

The information provided in this book is for informational purposes only and is not intended to be a source of advice or financial advice with respect to the material presented. The information contained in this book does not constitute legal or financial advice and should never be used without first consulting with a financial professional to determine what may be best for your individual needs.

Every effort has been made to contact and gain permission from each person mentioned in this book.

To my two precious little monkeys

Contents

Preface

Part I – Programming a Trader

1. The Origins of a Trader   10
Show Me the Bees and Honey

2. My Kind of Stocks   17
Bargain Buys & Catching Knives

3. An Introduction to Glitches   29
Arcade Mis-fire

4. More on Glitches   44
Leaky Pipes Means Trading's Ripe

5. My First Trades   52
A Career on the Cards

6. American Schooling   63
A Bettor Education

Part II – A Trading Journey

7. Starting Out as a Trader **Brokers and Broke Clients**	78
8. A World of Volatility and Change **Taking Scalps**	87
9. A Survival Guide for a Brutal Career **Serious Advice for Traders**	98
10. Missing and Taking Opportunities **Glitches Can't Buy You Love**	112
11. Bear Markets **Poland Calling**	122
12. A Final Blow **I.P.Ow!**	133
13. Raising the Stakes **C.R.E.A.M.**	143
14. Capitulation **ICOohhh!**	153
15. Cryptocurrency **Executive Decision**	163
16. A Return to Trading **Volatility to the Rescue**	173
Acknowledgements	185
Further Reading/Useful Resources	186

Welcome...

When I began writing this book four years ago, the ending I envisioned was quite different. It was a cliffhanger. Would the grizzled, struggling trading veteran–a relic from another time–find a way to survive and thrive in harsh markets overrun by ruthless automated trading robots?

Fortunately, thanks to my procrastination while writing, the book now has a happy ending. Although calling it a "happy ending" might be callous, considering the story ends with a pandemic ravaging the world and a brutal war being fought on my doorstep. However, in the cruel world of trading, these are just the types of events that typically translate into big profits for us traders.

So this book isn't quite a fairytale, but it is packed with adventure, drama, travel, romance, tragedy, and, ultimately, redemption. If I had to put the story into a single category, I would call it a "cautionary tale about my love affair with trading and risk."

My goal is to entertain, but I also want to educate–which meant when I started this book, I would be breaking my number one rule of trader education: Don't take advice from an impoverished trader. This rule is great in principle, but if we counted on wealthy and successful traders to provide us with our education, this space would be barren. Those traders have better things to do, like sailing their yachts, playing golf, and counting their cash, (although Instagram seems to be proving me wrong, spawning a peculiar breed that appears to have the yachts and fancy cars, but is also willing to share all of their secrets for a $50 chatroom subscription).

I granted myself an exception to this rule because I feel that I have a unique story to tell and some hidden industry secrets to share. I also have a valid excuse for not having enough cash to own a yacht; it's not because I don't know how to succeed, but because I have been too undisciplined to follow the known path to success. Therefore, instead of being one of those dime-a-dozen "how to make a million dollars in the stock market" type books, this is a cautionary tale that I believe gives a realistic insight into real life as a trader and what it requires to stay in the game long enough to be there when the good times arrive.

While motivated to write a book, staying motivated to write the book was another story, it was a constant struggle. Luckily, this struggle had a silver lining, or rather a golden lining, because my lack of motivation generally coincided with a spike in my trading profits. I began to enjoy writing, the creative aspects were a breath of fresh air after twenty-plus years of trading, but I still relished battling the markets, punching in and out of a few trades, and making thousands of dollars in the process. So when the markets and trading got hot, my pen got cold.

2020/2021 were turbulent years in the world, and the markets, bringing a continuous barrage of "writing distractions," meaning the book's narrative changed, its completion was delayed, and I finally had some cash to count.

Aware that I wrote mainly during the tough and challenging trading times, my goal isn't to fill the book full of doom and gloom. Being a professional trader can be a fantastic job: it's exhilarating stuff and provides freedom and independence. Of course, it can also make you filthy rich. I've experienced a fair share of that side of the profession in my twenty plus years in the business, and the book is sprinkled with fun stories about 20-year-olds in flip-flops making millions of dollars in a day. However, the reality is that this is a brutally tough profession, so I will warn you again, if you are looking for a sugar-coated, get-rich-quick type of book, you will be disappointed. In fact, the best advice I can give to the vast majority of wannabe professional traders is, "don't do it to yourself!" Hopefully, the stories, such as the one where–I am 40 years old, dead broke, my wife has just left me, and I'm moving back in with my dad in a small apartment in Poland—will provide enough deterrence.

For those that I can't scare off—or those just interested in learning more about trading—I'm confident I can provide insight that you won't find scouring the web or flipping through other trading books. I want to share the secrets of success I have learned myself and from the multitude of amazing traders I have had the pleasure of trading with. And I will give the reader an inside look into the firms we work for and the trading floors on which we congregate. I know this shadowy world of proprietary trading as well as anyone, having traded on a couple of the best floors in the business, and even owning a firm myself.

Outsiders will be shocked not only by the amount of money the top traders at these firms make but equally surprised by the approach they use to make their fortunes. Although we are equipped with a multitude of tools, and many of us focus on ultra-fast trading, I will be sharing lots of details about a magical approach that can bring success in any form of trading. And when I say any form of trading, I mean ANY form of trading: stocks, futures, crypto, eBay, market stalls, discount stores, etc.

Our journey to finding this magic will take us to some interesting places. We'll be spending time in schoolyard baseball card exchanges, with my mother digging through the discount clothes bins in British thrift stores, in the world's highest-action casinos in Macau and Vegas, at sketchy horse racing tracks in rural Texas, and in the HQ of an equally sketchy Polish crypto firm.

In each story, I hope to share some important lessons from both my successes and my failures. So, let's get started, in the only obvious place… the most miserable town in England.

Part I

Programming a Trader

1.

The Origins of a Trader:
Show Me the Bees and Honey

You might say that trading is in my roots. I am not sure if this is a blessing or a curse. It all depends on the day. Trading is the greatest job in the world when you are making money, and the worst when you are losing.

My roots spring from a town in southeast England named Grays. Ironically, the color with which the place shares its name pretty accurately captures the vibe. Grays recently earned the dubious distinction of being named England's "Capital of Misery", a title bestowed after receiving the lowest levels of life satisfaction in the country.

While Grays grapples with its miserableness, the County in which it sits, Essex, is riding a wave of popularity, thanks to the reality TV show "The Only Way is Essex". This highly addictive and light-hearted program has glamorized this traditionally downtrodden county—injecting a healthy dose of Hollywood glitz—and made it almost cool. The Essex Boys are portrayed as somewhat slicker versions of the lovable Dick Van Dyke character from the Mary Poppins film. But the Essex Girls are the real stars of the show; they are like an exotic species, identified by their loud and unusual lingo, bright orange tans, and fake boobs bursting from skin-tight dresses.

These aren't the same creatures I remember prowling the littered streets of Grays. The Essex of my youth was tough and gritty; full of working-class geezers with shaven heads and dodgy tattoos. I remember Essex girls clad in velvet tracksuits, chain-smoking and pounding cans of Stella Artois beer; not in high heels sipping champagne.

I know I'm not painting the rosiest picture of my Essex. In truth, it's home to mostly good, honest, and genuine people; it's real. I am proud to be from Essex, and who could blame it for being a little grimy when you consider all the abuse it has suffered from its big, noisy neighbor? London, which sits just a few miles west up the River Thames, has historically exploited its position and used Essex as little more than a dumping ground—literally discarding everything from dead bodies to human waste there. Further blemishing its already scarred landscape, Essex has been the chosen spot for London to spread its cheerless industrial sprawl and the toxic pollution that accompanies it.

In spite of all the drawbacks, its proximity to London has created plenty of jobs for the people of Essex. Traditionally these have been blue-collar laboring positions in factories and dockyards, but many from Essex have taken advantage of the fact that they live in the shadow of one of the financial capitals of the world. These opportunists have taken the unusual step of joining the white-collar world of finance, taking positions on the trading floors and in the pits of some of the biggest banks, brokerages, and exchanges in the world.

At first, this was unusual in the rigid class system of England. The world of finance is not a melting pot. London's prestigious and well-paid financial jobs are generally held by Oxford and Cambridge graduates, or others with glistening resumes and impressive pedigrees—not working-class geezers from Essex. However, some have smashed through this glass ceiling and landed these plum London trading jobs. It's part of a unique and symbiotic relationship between Essex and "The City" that has a fascinating origin story...

"The City" is an almost exact square-mile area that sits in the middle of London and at the heart of the world of finance. For the last couple of centuries, ambitious men (sadly trading has always been male-dominated) from Essex have been drawn to work as finance professionals on the trading floors. Nowadays, they make the daily commute every weekday morning in jam-packed commuter trains; then, in the evening, these same trains spit the exhausted bodies right back out to Essex.

When making this same pilgrimage myself, I always arrive in The City feeling a sense of awe, as if it is almost a religious experience. The stately-built banks and exchanges—most of which are centuries old—serve as cathedrals to the gods of capitalism. I enjoy watching the congregations of this celebrated religion navigate The City's ancient Roman footprint; the males are traditionally garbed in tailored pinstripe suits, and most are drawn to one of the area's hundreds of pubs to drink pints of their holy sacrament.

The ancient rituals endure, the old-school gentleman's way of doing business still pervades, and a sense of power seeps from every crevice in this gilded square mile. Therefore, it would seem that the daily interlopers from Essex would struggle to gain acceptance in this refined world; however, capitalism is the most inclusive of religions and is willing to turn a blind eye to each worshiper's class and bloodline. Of course, this inclusivity is only granted if the follower adheres to the number one and only commandment: Thou shalt make lots of money.

The trading pits of the numerous exchanges that dotted the city were the locations where many Essex men obeyed this commandment and were baptized as capitalists. This was an old-fashioned, face-to-face battleground where fancy degrees and impressive pedigree meant nothing, making it the perfect environment for those with a rough upbringing and a chip on their shoulder.

Today, the surviving physical exchanges of London serve as little more than monuments of a bygone era. The technological revolution has created seismic changes in the trading world. The battle is no longer in trading pits; instead, it takes place on computer servers and is fought between powerful computer algorithms. Although the method of trading has changed, these exchanges still hold their immense power: a merciful market offers us cheap gas, favorable exchange rates, and early retirement, while a vengeful market wipes out savings, jobs, and governments.

The trading industry has been flipped on its head during these last couple of decades, and armies of automated digital trading bots have risen. However, it seems that Essex traders still have their Midas touch. In 2020, for example, a truly astonishing story leaked out about a small group of independent traders working out of a nondescript office in the heart of Essex. During one truly mad day in April 2020, when the price of oil actually went negative, these Essex legends stepped in and took advantage of this glitch to the tune of $700 million. One 22-year-old trader made close to $100 million individually in a couple of hours!

So, traders from Essex mixed it in the pit with the privately-educated upper class over a century ago, and they are still battling elite trading bots right now. But why have there been so many traders from a traditionally blue-collar area where London dumps its waste? I have my own hypothesis, which is linked to another form of trading.

"Ello Luv! Cum git ya Uncle Reg. Spanish waiters, free for a nicker!"

You would be excused for thinking this is a nonsense language, but it is English. Granted, it may not be the King's English, but it is still something just as rich. This is Cockney, a truly unique dialect born in the working-class areas of East London. Although it is dying out, you might still hear the above phrase in one of the world-famous street London markets. Translated, it means, "Hello, madam. Would you like some vegetables? I have some potatoes for the price of 3 for one Pound".

Cockney's defining characteristic is its unique rhyming slang: veg becomes uncle Reg, and potatoes becomes Spanish waiters. So, while the traders (this is what the sellers are called) at these street markets have the same goal as any other type of trader—to make lots of money—they would rephrase it as "making bees and honey".

These colorful street markets and the lyrical and melodic Cockney spoken at them crept eastward over the years and invaded Essex, and are now an ingrained part of the local culture. The traders at the stalls have a legendary wit, but it's their trading skills and hustle that I truly admire.

A trader is defined as "someone who buys and sells goods", and regardless of the venue and the stock in trade, the aim for any trader is to buy low and sell higher. However, one could argue that these men pedaling vegetables are archetypical traders. Instead of sitting alone in front of a computer screen like most modern financial traders, these sellers are taking part in a face-to-face battle on the town square. It is trading in its rawest form and it's tough. Trades might be sealed with a wink and a smile instead of a click of a mouse button, but don't take the smile as a sign of softness; these street traders are hard and ruthless. They make a living by going up against dozens of other experienced and equally tough men every day, so there is room for a smile but little place for sentiment or self-doubt.

Of course, there are vast differences between trading in these street markets and trading the financial markets. Stock trading today has much more in common with solving a sudoku puzzle or programming than selling bananas on the street. The smooth-talking skills perfected by a street trader would be wasted on trying to charm a faceless trading algorithm, and I am sure that a pampered day trader would get eaten alive working a stall at a bustling street market in Essex. In fact, I think a couple of weeks working one of these stalls sounds like an excellent prerequisite for any prospective financial trader—there would at least be a lot fewer screaming heads on Twitter.

It's no surprise that, many decades ago, some of these street traders looked toward The City and fancied their chances in the cut-throat pits of the financial exchanges. They say, "a trader eats what he kills", and the men of Essex were more than willing to (at least metaphorically) kill to put food on the table. They were accustomed to (quite literally) taking shit from the city, to being thrown in the fire, to being abused… They had to build up thick layers of toughness and resilience just to survive life: two traits that just happen to be highly useful in the game of trading.

I may overly romanticize these street markets, but the fact remains that, indifferent to their class background, the doors to the lucrative world of London finance have always been open to those from Essex. Profit-hungry banks and brokerages long ago realized that class rules might not be applied the same in the trading world as elsewhere. People were judged solely on their performance. A working-class background and/or a limited education was tolerated in the trading world, as long as the cash was flowing in, of course. In many ways, this setting aside of class division in the ruthless pursuit of money was a blueprint for capitalism itself.

Nowadays, in the trading industry, a blind eye is turned to many more things than class or a Cockney accent. Nasty drug habits, unsociable working hours, and diva attitudes are all acceptable behavior if a trader is bringing in the cash. Corporate rules, office politics, and elaborate job evaluations mean little in this job; financial results are 100% quantifiable, and the trader's profits or losses

(P&L) tell the whole story. It is the judge, jury, and executioner. There are no gray areas.

2.

My Kind of Stocks: Bargain Buys & Catching Knives

I was born with Essex blood and an unquenchable thirst for risk pumping through my veins, so it would seem I was genetically predisposed to become a trader. Throw in the fact that my brother has been a professional trader his whole adult life, and you might assume that my parents have some connection to the markets or are, perhaps, gambling addicts. But no, neither my mother nor my father had a background in finance, and both shied away from thrill-seeking and gambling. My mom was a physical therapist, and my dad a transportation manager—two stable professions that are the polar opposites to the volatile world of day trading.

In fact, the only time I remember them briefly catching the trading bug was during the "dotcom bubble". My dad got his investment advice from a peculiar-sounding message board called "The Motley Fool", and my mother turned to another motley fool—her son, who was just starting out at a chop shop brokerage house—for advice. Needless to say, both stories ended badly; the tech bubble burst on my dad, while my mother never wanted to talk about the markets again after the tech mutual fund I put her 401K retirement savings into lost over 60% in a year.

In spite of this, I still believe that my brother, John, and I must have inherited the "trader" gene, as we both fell into the profession and have survived for what is an eternity in this brutal business. Who did we get it from? My guess is my mother. She didn't come from Essex, and she showed no interest in the markets, but I have a hypothesis that I believe backs up my suspicions. Before I get to it, I will first delve into a little about technical analysis. Don't worry, this will all tie together in the end, I promise...

As I write this, at the height of the 2020/2021 trading boom, it seems everyone has become filthy rich. I can't scroll through Twitter without being bombarded by self-proclaimed "rockstar traders" posting screenshots of their latest six-figure winner. Such tweets typically include a screenshot of a candlestick stock chart being gobbled up by the hottest new technical indicators, accompanied by another shot of the trader's daily profit gloriously stretching across the screen. The reader has to do the hard work of interpreting the noisy chart and assessing the authenticity of the accompanying profit.

[Of course, fast-forward to mid-2022, during a tough bear market, and a lot of these "rock stars" have strangely disappeared]

Interpreting charts—or what we call "technical analysis"—is defined by some as a science. The theory goes that if a trader can identify previous patterns, then they can predict others in the future. I wouldn't call myself a non-believer, but I do consider it more of an art than a science. And, like all art, the interpretation of a stock chart is open to the viewer. A piece of abstract modern art may bring a feeling of euphoria for some, while others may find it totally threatening. A stock chart may look bullish to you, but I might think that it indicates an immediate crash.

Theoretically, the interpreter is always right in technical analysis since some type of exotic technical indicator or moving average can always be presented to back up an argument. You may claim, "This chart shows this stock has formed a bullish pennant pattern, it's breaking its 20-day moving average and, therefore, it has momentum and is a screaming buy". I could then counter with, "Its last candle was a bearish engulfing Doji star, it's brushing the top of its Bollinger Band; it, therefore, is about to crash, so sell!" It's no wonder that when I scroll through charts on Twitter, I'm usually uncertain whether they are suggesting a buy or sell.

This is why I am more of a disciple of the science (others will call it an art) of tape reading. Tape reading is the somewhat ancient skill of analyzing order books, trades, and volume. This skill was glamorized by Jesse Livermore, author of the trading classic, *Reminiscences of a Stock Operator*. Since the book was written in the 1920s, many consider tape reading outdated in today's electronic markets. I disagree and find the real-time glimpse at the order flow of the market a lot more helpful than technical analysis when looking for short-term trades. I am obviously in the minority; most contemporary traders are fixated on technical analysis—an obsession fed to them by so-called "Trading Gurus" who, seemingly, do not know of, or are not willing to share, other more efficient and profitable ways to find winning trades.

Regardless of my skepticism about the science of technical analysis—as well as the mania surrounding it—at least half of the space on my own trading monitors is taken up by these charts. They are good risk management tools, and without these familiar green and red candlesticks, I feel like I'm flying blind. These charts are our eyes; they visualize the action for us. Don't get me wrong, charts are a valuable tool, but a tool that should be used in conjunction with other valuable tools available.

The other good thing about technical analysis is that anyone can do it. Some may call it a science, but there's no need for a fancy education; in fact, all you need to do is spend a lot of time staring at charts (I'd suggest without layers and layers of superfluous indicators), and you'll pick it up.

With time, each trader will be drawn toward certain technical setups that they feel a connection towards. With thousands of patterns and indicators to choose from, grouping traders based on these connections might seem impossible, but I have invented a method to separate traders into two distinct groups. In my world, you are either a "Bottom Picker" or a "Momentum Trader". I say distinct because it is extremely rare for a trader to fit into both categories. The ones who do are either lost or are the crème de la crème of traders.

Let me explain these two types of traders, and why this has anything to do with my mother.

Bottom Pickers seem to have a predisposition for punishment. It says a lot about this style of trading that all the proverbs are cautionary, such as "the bottom picker will end up with a stinky finger" or "don't catch falling knives". And, yes, I'm a grown man, but the name does still make me smirk!

A Bottom Picker is a trader who looks to buy technically weak stocks and ride the reversal back up. They are attempting to buy the bottom of a V- or U-shaped chart pattern. For example, let's say a stock that was trading at $50 has suddenly dropped $30, a Bottom Picker might spy a bargain. The next step is to find the correct entry point, usually indicated by when a level of support has formed. "Support", or a support level, refers to the price level that an asset does not fall below for a period of time; in other words, a price level with a lot of buyers.

If the trader has successfully identified the low point for the stock—i.e. picked the bottom—then he will make money as it bounces back up in price. However, if the stock breaks the support and keeps falling below the $30 buy-in price, the Bottom Picker needs to cut his losses or risk getting "a stinky finger".

Momentum Traders look at the market from a totally different angle. They are typically looking for strength, and they want to ride the momentum of a surge or breakout (an upward move outside a current price range). Instead of looking to buy support levels, they are searching for stocks that are reaching new highs and breaking through resistance levels. Resistance levels represent a technical level, or price, that an asset has had trouble exceeding in the time period being considered, or in other words, a price level with a lot of sellers.

Some Momentum Traders look to ride the momentum to the downside, shorting stocks as they break support, but the vast majority look for quality and strength. Since all the proverbs associated with momentum trading are very warm and fuzzy sounding, like "the trend is your friend", maybe this style makes more sense.

Now let me tell you more about my mother. She was an amazing woman; the kindest and smartest person I have known. She sadly passed away when I was in my mid-twenties, but I cherish my memories of her. I have even learned to look back fondly on the countless hours I spent as a child, bored out of my mind, waiting on her while she foraged through sales racks at her favorite stores. Shopping was her passion, but it wasn't because she was the 80s version of a fashionista—it was because she loved to bag bargains. Buying a dress for half of the price that someone else paid for it gave her the ultimate joy. Her closet served as a trophy cabinet for this hobby; it was lined with all the "bargains" she had bagged over the years, most of them unworn with the tags still on. It wasn't just clothing; she wouldn't spend a dollar unless she had searched first through her coupon collection. It was all a sport to her, and the actual deal was the ultimate prize.

I have followed in my mom's footsteps. Buying full-price clothing would be sacrilegious. There is no point in paying top dollar for a pair of jeans that will surely be cheaper if I just wait a while. The pricing in the market for clothes pretty much only goes one way, and that's down, so why buy at the top? I've followed my mom's mantra all my life.

Another area where I have never strayed from her teachings is in my trading. It seems I've never seen a beat-down, dirt-cheap stock I didn't want to bottom pick. My brother, John, is just the same, if not worse. Just like our mother loved getting a dress at 50% off, we feel the same way when we see a stock price getting cut in half. It's the exact same high.

There is also always a reason behind the price drop, whether it is a dress or a stock. That bright orange dress was on sale because it wasn't attractive; stocks also get unappealing when there is bad news or sentiment for that company or the market. Fortunately for my mother, she wasn't risking much money when she was bottom-picking unwanted dresses on a sales rack. Doing so in the financial markets is a much more treacherous game; one lapse of discipline and a falling knife can slice away a big chunk of your trading account.

Another thing I inherited from my mother was a contrarian streak. She never followed the masses, and neither do traders like myself. Momentum Traders go with the crowd: they look at a stock that others are buying and join in. Bottom picking is the ultimate act of contrarianism: we look at a stock that others think is weak—which is losing value because people are selling it off—and decide that they are wrong and that it should, in fact, be going up.

The contrarian investor argues that the crowd sometimes causes mispricings and provides opportunities for bargain hunters. It is about bargains, but it is often also about ego. This contrarian trader has the devilish tendency to crave the satisfaction of proving he is right and everything else is wrong. I often catch myself deviating from my trading plan, finding myself trying to pick the EXACT bottom of an obviously weak stock, with the goal of not only trying to bag the ultimate bargain but also seeking bragging rights for my immaculate timing.

Looking at it from a contrary view, bottom pickers aren't contrarian traders at all. In fact, our strategy, when executed correctly, is all about going with the crowd. The goal is to catch the exact moment when the momentum, or the crowd, switches from the sell side to the buy side. If the bottom picker times their entry correctly, they are one of the first to switch sides, enabling them to get a bargain bin price on their stock purchase. The risk is that the crowd doesn't join us, and in this case, the continued falling price—and the falling knife—cuts deep.

It's possible to have great success as either a Bottom Picker or Momentum Trader. Work out which tribe you belong to by reviewing your previous trades. They will tell you everything you need to know. You'll see where your expertise lies, and once you've reached that epiphany, you can adapt your trading strategies to your personality and strengths. Just don't battle human nature; stick with the side that suits you and your P&L the best.

Momentum trading and going with the flow probably makes more sense than trying to catch falling knives and reversals, but both styles offer monster-sized profits if timed and executed properly. Volatility is the trader's best friend, and this applies especially to Bottom Pickers. Volatility nearly always has an inverse relationship with the markets, so if the markets go down, the VIX index, which measures volatility, typically goes up. This made the market crashes of 2008 and 2020 the stuff of bottom-pickers dreams. There was so much to choose from, but if you stepped in too early and let your discipline stray, you were probably sliced up and unable to take advantage of some of the truly golden opportunities that arose when the market bottomed. In spite of a few flesh wounds, I was alive and kicking in 2008, and was able to take advantage of some amazing bottom-picking opportunities that accompanied this volatility tsunami. However, I still am haunted by the one giant fish that got away…

This painful story starts back in 2007, at a relatively peaceful and quiet time in the markets; so quiet, in fact, that I was taking regular trips to Las Vegas just to get an adrenaline supplement and quench my ever-present gambling thirst. Although quite costly (like most gamblers, I typically lost), these trips were both fun and something of an education.

My "experiences" in Vegas—in other words, my losses—opened my eyes to the brilliant business model under which casinos operate. Although I usually stuck to short-term trading, I decided it would be worth putting on a small position in my favorite casino stock, Las Vegas Sands ($LVS). It also seemed like the perfect hedge against my gambling losses—if I was going to stupidly lose money at the tables, I could invest a little smart money and make a profit as the casino thrived off the backs of suckers like me. My brother, John, and my good friend Mike had also compiled their own "field research" and agreed with my hypothesis; however, I became truly convinced of the potential of this trade when I visited Macau.

Loaded with what felt like a small fortune, freshly divorced, and needing a break from trading, I set off on an adventure in early 2008. My goal was to circumnavigate the globe. I started in London and made my way through Europe to Egypt. After some sightseeing and enjoying the beautiful beaches of the Sinai Peninsula, I headed to Thailand to meet some friends and blow off plenty of steam. I then went to India to cleanse myself of all that partying.

After a month of semi-roughing it and attempting to get all spiritual, I was in dire need of some Western-style comfort, so I made a beeline to Hong Kong. It was a relief to get back to air conditioning and room service, but what I had really missed was the risk, adrenaline, and dopamine hit of making trades. Without even a laptop to trade from (this was in a bygone era when every trader wasn't joined at the hip with a laptop), I went seeking the next best thing and jumped a ferry for the short ride to Macau and its bright lights and casinos.

I first made my way to the enormous Venetian Casino, which is owned by Las Vegas Sands, but it didn't take long to realize that Macau and Vegas have little in common. In Vegas, gambling is the main attraction, but extravagant shows, fancy bars and clubs, wild pool parties, and other hedonistic activities offer a welcome distraction from the gaming tables. In Macau, I saw people doing one thing, and one thing only, and that was gambling. Searching for a bar, I passed table after table of zombie-like gamblers throwing away fortunes; the average bet seemed double the size of what you would typically see in Vegas.

I eventually found a bar, and after lubricating myself up, I immediately scratched my itch by getting into the action, but the thrill was quickly replaced by the unpleasant and familiar sensation that comes with losing lots of money. For me, this feeling seems to feel a lot sharper when gambling rather than trading. Even after 20 years in the game, a bad losing day as a trader still hurts, but the pain doesn't relate to the actual financial loss—instead, the frustration comes more from being disappointed in one's own performance. What's more, a bad day trading can be a wake-up call that leads to some tough self-analysis and helps you pull yourself together and be better next time. But knowing the house holds the edge, losing money in a casino just feels like a fool's game!

At least I left with some valuable intel: Macau wasn't the place to come to party, and the Las Vegas Sands company ($LVS) owned a huge casino that was relieving some of the world's hardest gamblers of absolute fortunes.

From Hong Kong, I headed eastward and met up with my cohorts, John and Mike, in Austin. I shared my intel, and John, Mike, and I immediately started buying small chunks of $LVS stock. Unfortunately, our timing was awful because it was the summer of 2008, and the markets were beginning to crash. Buying $LVS on the dips came naturally to this bottom picker, but I choose to abandon the "cutting the loser" part of the bottom picking creed, essentially becoming a Dollar-cost averaging investor. I just added $LVS shares every time it sold off, but it was too early to be doing bargain shopping, and time after time I was punished. This wasn't the time to buy anything, the market was cratering, and the world's financial system was on the brink of collapse. Casinos are a great business model, but when everybody is scared shitless, even a great business inevitably suffers. $LVS got creamed! There was even talk of bankruptcy, and the stock sold off from $140 in late 2007 to $1 in early 2009!

This move from $140 to $1 in just over a year was a great example of capitulation. Capitulation describes a state of panic in an asset or market; it's the moment when beat-up investors can't take anymore, so they throw their hands up in surrender and sell whatever they have. It creates an extremely oversold situation where the price of the asset doesn't reflect the underlying fundamentals. Capitulation is a genuine example of mispricing and is one of the cases when the crowd is wrong, and the stock is worth more than its underlying price. It is every bottom picker and contrarian's dream.

Capitulation is a rare event, but in 2008 and 2009, it was happening everywhere. The whole stock market basically capitulated and, for a skilled bottom-picker—or semi-skilled one like myself—this presented tremendous opportunities. It's tough to act rationally in such a volatile market because even what seems like a good trade can be harshly punished. However, with the right mindset and the willingness to endure a little short-term pain, there are some opportunities of a lifetime.

Buying $LVS when it dropped to $1 in early 2009 seemed like a no-brainer; it was a great company in a strong sector, and even if it had gone bankrupt, the stock would have been worth something. It was truly at rock bottom, because there was almost nowhere lower to go, offering a potentially huge reward, for what seemed like little risk.

Of course, a few months earlier when $LVS crashed from $140 to $10, we thought there was little risk, figuring that there couldn't be many investors left who hadn't already given up and cashed in their chips. We thought wrongly, in no time at all we were down 90% on our $10 buys.

I don't know if we were tough, stubborn, or optimistic, or if we had just done our homework and believed in the business, but we didn't sell. In fact, when $LVS reached $1, we felt that there was nothing left to lose, so despite our stinky fingers, we all loaded in and bought anywhere from 20k to 50k shares each. The CEO of $LVS seemed to agree with our assessment, because he joined us and stepped in and bought millions of shares. This news helped the stock stabilize, then the panic gradually subsided, and the market rebounded.

It didn't take too long for $LVS to bounce up to $5, representing a healthy 500% return from our $1 buys. My mentality as a very short-term trader—or what you would call a 'scalper'—makes it really tough, if not impossible, for me to hold long-term positions. I, therefore, started to cover some of my position for around $5. I had nearly been destroyed by the market action of that past year, and was truly shell-shocked, so I was happy to just be making some profit on the trade and recouping some losses.

I sold the rest of my position between $5 and $10, thankful for the nice pop, and happy and relieved to have some nice profits from my $1 buys. John and Mike played it a lot cooler than trigger-happy me, they sat back and rode the surge like skilled momentum traders and were rewarded for their patience with a truly monster payday. Within a year, they were sitting on a stack of $LVS worth fifty times more than the buy-in price!

Inevitably, since I have been trading for twenty years, there are plenty of other "one that got away" tales. Since I'm a bottom-picker, the trades like the $LVS one hurt the most, but I've also missed out on some amazing momentum trades. Back in 2016, my good friend Chris was imploring me to buy Bitcoin and Ethereum, which he said were "the next big thing". I was interested in these strange new Cryptocurrencies, but my enthusiasm quickly faded when I saw the charts. Bitcoin had recently doubled in price, and Ethereum had just moved from $1 to $7, a 700% move! Being a Bottom Picker, I concluded that I was way too late to the party. In fact, I would have shorted them if I could have.

A Momentum Trader would have taken one look at the huge green candles littering the chart and jumped straight in to join the surge. It would have been quite a ride too! Ethereum went to $1,500 within 2 years, and Bitcoin went to $20,000! To be honest, I wasn't too upset at missing out because momentum trading just isn't in my DNA. I'm a bargain hunter, like my mother—and I only shop at stores where the bargains are at rock-bottom prices.

Over the years, I've chosen my tribe, and I understand my strengths and weaknesses. I don't have skills in momentum trading. Even if I had bought Ethereum at $7, I would have sold it as soon as it hit $15 and patted myself on the back for doubling my money. It's probably a blessing that I missed out because, as every trader knows, the pain of covering a winner too early is so much worse than the pain of not investing at all.

3.

An Introduction to Glitches: Arcade Mis-fire

The stories from Las Vegas and Macau bring back fond memories, but I haven't returned to either in years. I might still appreciate that addictive buzz a happening casino floor provides, but since the casino holds the all-important "edge" or advantage over the player, I have come to accept these casino games are fool's games. As traders, we are taught to avoid any strategy that lacks an edge, or an advantage over the market, so why would a trader play a casino game knowing they are the fool? In this chapter, I will explore whether it is possible for a gambler to turn the tables and wrestle that edge away from the casino. I will argue yes, and that a prepubescent child can even do it. This leads me to the following story; a tale that backs up this argument, chronicles my introduction to gaming, and provides some very valuable lessons about trading...

As a young boy growing up in Essex, I was lucky enough to have some family living in the charming little seaside town of Broadstairs, located in the neighboring county of Kent on the southeast coast of England. Our family would make annual trips there for a traditional English summer holiday: a nice beach, amazing fish and chips, mouth-watering ice cream, bad weather, and a couple of amusement arcades.

How do I describe an amusement arcade for non-British readers? It's basically a playground with machines full of flashing lights. There are pinball machines, shoot-em-ups, sports games, and fighting games, and then there are slot machines. And there is not often demarcation; the innocent games for kids are positioned right next to the poker machines that attract hard adult gamblers.

The fact that nobody seems bothered by this is a good indication of just how deeply gambling is ingrained into British culture. There are numerous bookmaking shops in every small town, and even sports stadiums have their own bookies—so it makes sense that gambling is an essential part of many people's family holidays. In fact, the arcade is the first spot that most children, or compulsive gamblers, rush to visit on a trip to the seaside.

The other thing to note about most arcades that I visited as a kid was that the place was supervised by a disinterested teenager in a booth in the corner whose only responsibility was to break notes into change that could be fed into the machines. Nobody was policing the joint to check who was using which machines.

Around the age of 10, I was granted the freedom to venture out to the arcades alone during our visits to Broadstairs. Left to my own devices, it didn't take long for a dark and compelling force inside me to pull me away from the video games and towards the sweet sound of pound coins pinging out of slot machines. Sure, the video games were fun, but winning cold hard cash seemed even more enticing. It seemed like these games were even targeted at kids, each of them covered with bright flashing lights and cartoonish characters. I can still remember the buzz of shoving a ten-pence coin into the first slot machine I stumbled upon, hoping to win big.

Once transformed into a prepubescent gambler, it was quickly drawn to a certain electronic horse racing game that regularly called out "Place your Bets!" in a hypnotic 80s robotic voice. The game was so simple to play that even a 10-year-old gambling novice could figure it out. The player picked one of five horses in a race, with each horse having different odds of winning, starting at 2 to 1 (bet 1 to win 2), and working the way up to 10 to 1.

I went through a few Pounds, trying bets on different horses without any luck. Then, finally, I bet on horse number 2 and backed a winner at odds of 5 to 1. Imagine, my first winning bet! The very first shot of dopamine my brain ever received from a winning bet or trade. It was a pretty defining moment in my life.

Figuring that you should stick with the winners, I bet on the number 2 in the next race and, lo-and-behold, I won again! I became buzzed out of my tiny little mind on dopamine and just kept on sitting there, shoving in coins and backing number 2 every race. I did lose my fair share, but I was winning far more often than 20% of the time. I didn't have advanced statistical analysis skills back then, but I somehow realized that if you have a greater than 20% winning rate on a 5 to 1 bet, assuming you are risking the same amount each time, you WILL make money.

This is exactly how I evaluate a potential trade today: what is my risk, what is my reward, and what is the probability of success. In trading, calculating these variables, especially the reward part, is a lot tougher, but they were concretely defined in the horse racing game. I knew exactly my risk and reward—and the fact that my shorts were being tugged to the ground by the weight of hard-won one-pound coins confirmed that this strategy had an 'edge'.

I did this every day on that holiday—always betting on the number 2 horse—and found that my success was replicated each time. I'd earned a small fortune for such a small boy, and I was hooked. I figured at this rate I would be a millionaire before I was a teenager... if only I didn't have to go back home to school in Essex after a week!

I had to wait a full year to return to Broadstairs. It was agonizing, considering I was on the verge of becoming filthy rich. Upon my arrival the following summer, I sprinted to the arcade and started pouring coins into my lucky horse racing game. I followed my strategy of betting on horse number 2 every time, but this time it was paying off far less than 20% of the time. I quickly burned through 5 Pounds, then 5 more. I sensed it wasn't going to plan—but stubbornness and lack of discipline have been lifelong character defects—so, of course, I returned to the arcade that evening and burned through another 15 pounds.

This final act of desperation was the prepubescent version of a strategy I still revert to in times of despair—one that is widely known as "revenge trading." It's when a trader tries to reverse (or revenge) a loss, not by adjusting or changing a losing strategy, but by just saying "fuck it" and betting bigger. Not surprisingly, the end result often mirrors my last stand at the arcade: losing everything.

I am not sure what ended the good times, perhaps other gamblers had discovered this bug. If a skilled gambler, or any half-intelligent opportunist, had discovered this glitch, they would have taken full advantage of it, shoveling the maximum bet into the machine each time. If this had happened, I'm sure the suspicions of the arcade management would have been raised. Granted, the management of this arcade had a laissez-faire attitude when it came to certain things—such as child gambling—but I'm sure they would have become instantly more engaged if they saw that one of their machines was bleeding money. They would, no doubt, have decommissioned or recalibrated the machine to close the loophole. Whatever happened, the good times were over for one ten-year-old kid, and my dreams of becoming a millionaire in increments of 5 pound payouts from an arcade game were dashed.

Despite the sad ending, Britain's negligent gambling safeguards allowed me to stumble upon an invaluable lesson—one which is still what I would call the perfect approach to both gambling and trading. It's a philosophy that few follow and one that is barely mentioned when scouring through trader "educational material" on the internet or in other books. And yet, this secretive world has provided me, and the majority of the traders I know, with a lion's share of our trading profits.

I'm talking about FINDING A GLITCH! It's what accidentally happened to me in Broadstairs and is the most effective way to succeed in trading. Make no mistake, this is the most valuable nugget of advice that I can share with you.

I will use the word "glitch" to describe a malfunction, mispricing, arbitrage, or inefficiency within a market. Simply put, it's "something that shouldn't be there." Glitches prove that markets aren't efficient, and that they do often break, crack or leak. When the markets "break", it's truly the most efficient time to make money. Lots of money. If one of these glitches can make it easy for a child to beat the house in a casino, imagine what a skilled trader in a trillion-dollar market can do after noticing a crack in the system.

The strategies that take advantage of these glitches don't rely on speculation, technical or fundamental analysis, or hoping and praying that markets go up or down. "I think", "I feel", and "I hope" are the most dangerous phrases in trading, but you would never hear them uttered from the lips of a skilled glitch trader, instead the glitch trader operates mechanically and thinks of themselves not as some sly financial wizard who predicts the next move in markets, but as more of a hacker looking for ways to exploit what's broken in the markets.

This world of glitches seems secretive, but most traders are usually well versed in legendary glitch trading tales such as the one I shared earlier about the

Essex oil traders who took advantage of a crash in oil prices. It is a textbook example of a glitch trade; the market broke, the price of oil went negative, then these young men saw the glitch, stepped in and made tens of millions each. Another epic glitch trading tale happened just upriver from Essex and involved one of my trading heroes, Nav Sarao. Nav made hundreds of millions preying on glitches in the futures markets while trading out his bedroom in his parent's house. Nav was so good at his job, that he ultimately became the fall guy for the Flash Crash of 2010. The book *Flash Crash*, by Liam Vaughan does a great job telling this story. The legendary GameStop short squeeze of 2021 is one more sensational example of what I would call a glitch.

Stories like these provide inspiration for all traders, but why don't the masses follow these lessons and do things the easier, more efficient, and more lucrative way? The main culprit is the sketchy world of trader education. The sources that most traders count on for their education would rather bombard their audience with hype and hyperbole on how to get filthy rich while trading some exotic candlestick pattern. In the last 15 years, I have seen traders that I personally know make 100s of millions of dollars executing strategies revolving around the opening and closing auctions on the stock exchanges, but I challenge you to find any "trader educational sources" touting these lucrative strategies.

If these glitches offer the easiest path to riches, why are they a secret, and why are these strategies being trumpeted on Twitter and YouTube, and in trading books? Firstly, your favorite "guru" is probably not in on this secret. I hate to break the news, but many of these superstar traders aren't as successful as they seem. I don't want to paint the entire trader education space with the same brush because there are definitely some helpful resources out there; however, in a world where making millions is the sign of success, you have to be skeptical when a "successful" trader is spending all their time on social media and busting their ass trying to sell a $50-per-month subscription service.

Let's assume that this "guru" is in on the secret, and that pic of him driving the Lamborghini is legit. Well, just like it would have been against my own best interest to tell anyone else about the glitch on the horse racing arcade game, it is against the "gurus" best interest to share the juicy details of a trading glitch. Crowds are kryptonite for most glitch strategies. The more people that know, the faster it disappears, and the good times end.

The trader may not have to worry about pesky arcade management negating a glitch; instead, he is battling other traders and algorithms, which are all trying to get a piece of a pie that is continually shrinking in size. Therefore, with a lucrative glitch strategy potentially bringing in hundreds of thousands, if not millions of dollars, it makes sense that a trader in possession of such a strategy would focus on milking the strategy, not flogging it online and thus overcrowding the trade.

I was lucky enough to start my trading career in an office teeming with glitch hunters, but not surprisingly, my coworkers were quite guarded with their winning strategies. I still got the gist of where the "easy money" was, and–after $40,000 in initial losses–I finally got the hang of it and have never since turned my back on these wonderful strategies that have provided me with the meat of my trading profits. This office of mine wasn't, and isn't, the only one in on the secret. I know of many offices packed full of traders doing things the easy way and gobbling up the profits provided by glitches. What's more, the giant high-frequency trading and quantitative hedge funds glitch hunt on an industrial scale. They don't just gobble, they truly gorge themselves. Firms such as Citadel and Renaissance make billions in automatizing these types of strategies.

These glitches are not just available to equity traders, but are waiting to be exploited in all markets. I talk to futures traders and options traders who rely on glitches, and the Cryptocurrency markets were kind enough to provide me with one of my most efficient strategies. It's not only financial traders feasting; my bottom-picking mother was a glitch hunter! One of her favorite strategies was taking advantage of mispricings (a more common phenomenon back in the days before bar codes on price tags). eBay and similar marketplaces are also teeming with glitch hunters looking for suckers, and I personally proved that finding a glitch at a casino can literally be child's play.

Once the door has been opened to this magical world and the trader grasps the true potential of these types of strategies, the next step is the radical adjustment of the trading mindset. Delusions of grandeur about being part of the world of high finance must be swept aside; most efficient day traders are akin to scavengers, picking up the scraps that big players leave behind.

Before I completely dive in, I want to express that—while I firmly believe that these glitch strategies are the most efficient way for active traders to make money in the markets—it is still imperative to have a grasp of the traditional fundamentals of trading, such as technical analysis, tape reading, trading psychology, and so on.

Firstly, the trader needs this understanding to find and execute these glitch strategies. Without plenty of screen time, a firm understanding of market mechanics, and a strong head, a trader will typically fail even if they have been handed the keys to the kingdom. Although, I will add a disclaimer that sometimes—on the rarest of occasions—these strategies have so much edge that even an unskilled newbie can make millions (and I'll cover one such example in the next chapter).

Secondly, these strategies are used most effectively in conjunction with traditional trading strategies because these glitches are rare and often only briefly exist. It can take months to find one of these lucrative strategies, so backup streams of trading income are needed. As I illustrated in the previous chapter, it's quite possible to make plenty of money using more traditional strategies, and many traders do just that. My goal here is to open your eyes to an additional set of strategies that can offer a far superior edge when executed properly.

Here are some of my favorite glitches from the past.

The Hunger Games

This "rookie sniping strategy" is not only a great example of a glitch strategy; it also illustrates how ruthless the trading business is. This strategy was my introduction to glitches and served as a baptism by fire into the world of trading.

It was what we might call an arbitrage strategy. Arbitrage is the holy grail of glitches, if not the whole world of trading. It allows the trader to take advantage of price differences between different markets and exchanges, and when done correctly, it offers what we traders call "free cash". Arbitrage has become tougher to find in today's electronic markets, but it was a lot easier to come by before automated trading took over.

When I was starting out, all the separate exchanges that traded U.S stocks were not linked together like they are now, so on one exchange, a buyer might be trying to buy XYZ stock at $10.25, and then on another exchange, a sucker–sorry, I mean seller–might step in and try to sell XYZ at $10.00. It doesn't take a genius to realize that this market fragmentation presents an opportunity for a skilled glitch trader, or arbitrager.

The savvy veteran traders at my first trading job would wait for that sucker to offer XYZ stock at $10. They would quickly buy in and then immediately sell on the other exchange at $10.25, for a quick .25 cents of free cash.

They were taking advantage of the exchange arbitrage to make these lucrative trades, but also of the inexperienced traders, such as myself, who were often supplying the bait.

At the proprietary trading firm, Zone Trading (which is now Kershner Trading) in Austin, Texas, I sat together with the rest of the wide-eyed rookies on one side of a highly segregated office; on the other side sat the savvy veteran traders. Some of my first, but not fondest, memories of trading were watching those guys sitting frozen with their eyes glued to their gigantic old-school CRT monitors. Their itchy trigger fingers—which had been conditioned by countless kills while playing their favorite 1PP shooter games—would hover over their keyboards.

We rookies would go about our business on our side, eagerly learning the ropes of our exciting new profession. Inevitably though, one of us would make a slip on the keyboard and place a bid or offer that was out of whack with the other exchanges, thus offering a juicy scrap for our "co-workers". When that erroneous order would hit the exchange, a feeding frenzy would ensue. The thundering sound of fingers pounding on keyboards would wail from the veterans' side, followed by an eerie silence and then a scream of agony from the hapless rookie trader who was caught in the trap.

This cruel game, where your supposed "teachers and mentors" preyed on your every mistake, provided quite an eye-opening introduction to the world of trading. However, I somehow survived this trial by fire, and I am proud to tell you that I never adopted this cold-blooded strategy when I became a veteran (I was way too slow on the keyboard to compete for the scraps).

Auction Order Strategy

By breaching the glitch-trader's time-honored code of secrecy, and revealing this next strategy, I may incense a few of my peers. I'll tread carefully and will not divulge all the secrets, but I can't talk about glitch strategies without mentioning the one strategy that has probably provided for at least half of the profits of every successful equity trader I have known over the last 20 years. These auctions are also something that every active equity trader should be aware of. It's no surprise that this secret is guarded like the Crown jewels. In fact, when I mention the world of opening and closing auctions to traders outside my circle, I usually get a blank stare and expressions of shock that everyone isn't making all their cash trading using fancy candlestick technical setups like the guy on the YouTube video brags about.

Auction strategies revolve around a single aggregated trade that happens at the open and close of the U.S. stock markets (NYSE and NASDAQ) in each individual stock. This auction is typically for the benefit of big players who want to buy, or dump, large quantities of shares. I won't get too technical, but the goal is to build strategies that take advantage of this large aggregated twice-daily auction. I would encourage every equity trader to familiarize themselves with how these auctions work, not only because they offer ample trading opportunities, but also because they are an important part of the market structure.

One great example happened right before Christmas in 2020, when Tesla was to be added to the S&P 500 index. This meant that millions of shares of Tesla would be bought by the numerous funds that mimic this index, and the last day for these funds to buy Tesla was on Friday, 18th December. Although these funds had weeks to buy shares before Tesla was added to the index, many waited until literally the last minute and used this closing auction to buy the remaining shares they needed. Therefore, with one minute left before the close of trading, the Nasdaq market indicated that there were 17 million more shares to be bought than to be sold (a buy imbalance) on this auction.

Seconds before the close of trading, smart traders bought in at somewhere between $640 and $660, and then immediately offered (sold) their shares to this auction. Most of us auction veterans expected this to be a good trade, but we were blown away when the auction price was $695. These smart, and somewhat lucky traders had made around $50 per share in only a few seconds, and with just a couple of clicks of the mouse.

I should hold my hands up and say that I wasn't one of them. I was a little frightened by the high price of Tesla and its volatility. To put it lightly, it was a decision I regretted when a couple of my peers made more money in those 30 seconds than I had made in the last 15 years of trading. Fortune favors the brave, I guess.

VXX Glitch

Another glitch strategy I have used in the past involved $VXX, a volatility-tracking ETN (exchange trading note). It's been one of my favorite stocks to trade over the years, so I have always kept a close eye on its trading action. When the market gets volatile, this volatility ETN naturally fluctuates more. Back in 2014, when the volatility in the market spiked, I noticed a pattern that seemed too good to be true. From exactly 3:14 pm to 3:15 pm, during the after-hours trading session, this stock would have a quick move to the upside, which was unrelated to the market action. It doesn't take a genius to figure out how to profit from this glitch; buy VXX at 3:14 pm and then sell at 3:15 pm. Two clicks of the mouse, and one minute of my time, was all it took to execute one of the most successful trading strategies of my career.

I later learned this spike was happening because of a quirk in the rebalancing of VIX futures, but ultimately the "why" doesn't matter, the important thing after discovering a glitch is to formulate a strategy as quickly as possible and then execute. As with most of these glitch strategies, this one only worked for a short period, maybe a year, so it's imperative to put your foot on the gas when it's working, but it's just as important to be ready to apply the brakes once it stops.

Bitcoin Arbitrage

A good arbitrage strategy is one that offers a superior edge and is simple to execute: buy on one exchange at a low price, and sell on another for a higher price. An excellent example was an inter-exchange arbitrage opportunity involving Bitcoin in 2017 and 2018.

The cryptocurrency markets were crazy at this time, and Bitcoin was prone to wild price fluctuations. Since Bitcoin isn't traded on a centralized exchange, the insane action was spread among multiple exchanges. This market fragmentation proved to be very inefficient, resulting in huge price differences between exchanges, providing an environment ripe for opportunist arbitrage traders. It was as simple as buying Bitcoin on one exchange for perhaps $5000, and then transferring it to another exchange and selling at perhaps $5500. While simple and effective, there was a little risk. Sometimes it would take up to half an hour for the transfer to process, and during these wild times, there was a chance that the price could swing against you. However, if the price difference was big enough, it was definitely a risk worth taking.

eBay Assassin

As I said earlier, glitches happen in all markets, and online marketplaces such as eBay offer ripe pickings for savvy traders. I have my own glitch story from the Polish version of eBay. This humbling experience began when I inadvertently advertised some computer monitors for sale at a ridiculously low price. Within minutes of posting this ad, a buyer was at my door with a handful of cash and a cheeky smirk on his face. After the buyer split the scene of the crime with monitors in hand, I started to get a little suspicious, so minutes later I checked the website to see what similar monitors were being sold for, and to my shock and horror, saw my monitors back on the market at a 50% premium.

I compare this glitch hunter to those veterans who provided me with my introduction to glitches at that first office of mine. This guy who showed up at my door was using the same strategy as those parasites; look for an errand offer, hit it quickly, and get the hell out. This guy even had the balls to come to my own house. I have to admit that I was disappointed in being on the wrong side of the trade, but I wanted to congratulate him on one hell of a trade.

I could keep on listing glitch strategies: the airline flight that was mispriced at only $1 online, the wager that was placed before the bookie had time to update his odds after a major injury to the star quarterback. These are all examples from the past, and a good glitch strategy disappears fast, so my goal isn't to hand out golden glitch strategies, it isn't that easy, and unfortunately, I am not that charitable. Instead, I hope to provide a roadmap and leave the challenge of finding these winning lottery tickets to you, the reader, but I can at least guarantee they are out there, and will offer further guidance in your quest throughout the book.

You might reject this mission, and say, "I'm not interested in trading like this, I want to be a proper trader who relies on technical and fundamental analysis." That's fine, but I want to point out how the majority of successful traders I know make a big portion of their profits, and the type of strategies that we found offer the greatest edge. Ultimately, I want to open the reader's eyes to an approach to trading, i.e., buying and selling things, that is usually the most efficient method whether you are buying an S&P futures contract or a computer monitor.

Even if you prefer other more "glamorous" forms of trading, the aim of the game is to make as much money as possible. My advice would be to follow the path that would give you the best chance of achieving that goal, especially as the luxury of consistently making money from your preferred style of trading is rarely afforded.

4.

More on Glitches: Leaky Pipes Means Trading's Ripe

Being a trader is akin to owning a funeral parlor; our fortunes depend on the misery of others. We are the ambulance-chasers of the financial world. Terrorist attacks, pandemics, and recessions are the moments when we see huge spikes in our trading profits. It's not a particularly pleasant predicament to rely on everyone else's distress for your own financial prosperity, but it's the unsavory reality of the life we have chosen.

Nearly all skilled traders relish fear—and the market volatility that it causes—but a glitch trader truly makes hay when the sun isn't shining for others. All traders want movement in the markets, but glitch traders relish fear. This breed thrives when markets are shaken to their very foundations and are struggling to meet their ultimate goal, which is to match buyers and sellers in a "fair and orderly manner".

Sudden market volatility typically causes a seismic shock, which can have two consequences: either there is a flurry of activity and volume in the market, or market participants get scared shitless and run for the hills, resulting in a lack of liquidity. Either scenario puts an enormous strain on the inner plumbing of the market. The pipes (or what are now fiber optic cables) that connect the market participants, then either get clogged with too many trades or become bone dry from a lack of orders. In either condition, these pipes leak or crack eventually, causing the market to become unorderly and inefficient. In this scenario, a skilled glitch trade will be waiting with a big old bucket to catch all the cash flowing from the broken pipes.

Typically, a bucket does the job, but—back in 2008, when the global financial markets were on the brink of collapse—you could have filled swimming pools with all the money flowing from the glitches. Unfortunately for me, I was holding the equivalent of a shot glass when this volatility tsunami hit. I had just left Texas for London and was attempting to navigate the wildest markets I have ever seen with antiquated dial-up internet out of the dining room of my Victorian apartment.

My brother John and my old crew back in Texas were not exactly Wall Street types, but they at least had an office to trade from. This nondescript office, hidden in a suburban office park in Austin, Texas, housed a bunch of unshaven, 20-something-year-olds who had a penchant for working shirtless and for pulverizing computer keyboards. Booming hip hop and screams of agony and ecstasy typically rattled the walls, startling the 'civilians' in the neighboring offices. So, maybe "professional" isn't the best way to describe the setup, but this motley crew did at least have comradery and high-speed internet.

If markets are slow, trading results tend to suffer. The couple of years prior to 2008 were tough trading years, and the population of the Texas office had dwindled as people moved on. Although, the top traders in the office typically always found a way to make good money. Before 2008, making good money meant consistent four-figure profit days—which isn't a bad living for a twenty-something. However, once 2008 hit, even those less skilled rookie traders who had been struggling to keep their heads above water suddenly found themselves swimming in money. Many became instant millionaires.

You might assume that these riches were made by shrewdly shorting stocks and taking advantage of the over 50% decline in most markets. We were fed this narrative by best-selling books written by, or written about, the legendary trading savants who deftly predicted the housing market's collapse back in 2008. It makes sense, makes for great reading, and provides us with the narrative that trading is about thumbing through pages of research and numbers, looking for that golden nugget of data that foretells the future. Other books, and most of the screaming heads on Twitter, tell us that technical analysis is the tool that professionals rely on to take advantage of the big moves in the markets–just hop on that downward trendline and ride that wave of momentum to easy riches.

However, these rookies in Texas–some of whom had never even had a profitable trading month–didn't become instant millionaires in 2008 because they stumbled on some exotic candlestick technical pattern, and most of them wouldn't have known how to even calculate a PE ratio. Instead, these traders hit the jackpot because the market was under tremendous strain, pipes were bursting, and one of the guys in the office discovered an amazing glitch strategy and was nice enough to share his secret.

This kind trader had stumbled upon a secret closing market auction order; the same type that I mentioned in the last chapter that has long been a cash cow for most of the equity traders I know. While the strategy I described before took advantage of an out-of-the-money trade on the NYSE or Nasdaq exchanges, this particular trader discovered a similar glitch on a smaller exchange. To partake in this auction, you needed special data feeds that few had, or ever knew existed. Armed with these feeds and holding the blueprint to this secret strategy, a trader could make millions in a few seconds and with just a couple of quick keystrokes. Fortunately, the volume and liquidity in this auction was extremely heavy, so it was possible for everyone in the office to join in on the fun.

There was a catastrophe or two mixed in with this fun. One such incident occurred on a day when the office was loaded into this trade, and music was playing so loud that it drowned out some market-moving news being broadcast by the news service. It's safe to say the music subsequently was played more quietly after the news caused the trade to go against them, ultimately costing the office millions of dollars!

John passed this golden strategy over to me in London, but I can't blame loud music for my poor performance. My excuse had more to do with stubbornness (later in the book I'll go into the tragic details). Suffice to say, the traders in the Texas office weren't as stupid as me and churned out millions in profits during late 2008. Even traders who had never tasted a profitable month were transformed from broke flip-flop-wearing dudes into millionaire flip-flop-wearing dudes in weeks.

I must clarify, not every trader in that office hit the jackpot. Without proper execution, a good glitch is worthless, but for the traders with courage and discipline they might have been handed out winning lottery tickets; that was how lucrative this strategy was. This type of generosity is also not common in the business. Most other traders aren't so kind about sharing their golden secrets. I have seen physical altercations break out over such strategies. When I was a rookie, my coach—who was being paid to teach me how to trade—would actually turn off his computer monitors when he would go to the bathroom, fearing I might steal his glitch secrets.

It makes sense that traders protect their glitch secrets when sharing might cut into their share of profits. However, if someone is feeling very generous, or being particular naive, they might let them slip. I've even unearthed a glitch secret on YouTube in the past—which I will share later on—that saved me from destitution and resurrected my trading career.

I'm pretty sure that secret was shared more out of naivety than anything else (so don't count on YouTube and Twitter for the source of your trading strategies, even if they can be great sources to generate ideas). However, I prefer to think that it was kindness and not naivety that made the trader in the Texas office share the wealth. I like to believe that he thought his generosity would be repaid. That is one of the many unmeasurable benefits of working in collaboration with a group of fellow traders. You don't expect to be handed a winning lottery ticket like those lucky souls in that Texas office were handed back in 2008, but the cooperation, collaboration, and competition that come with working within a healthy group are invaluable.

Being handed, or stealing one of these cash-printing glitch strategies is the easiest way to riches, but you can't wait around for the moment that someone hands you a winning lottery ticket. Good traders need to try to uncover a glitch for themselves. Although it is the hard way, discovering and formulating a winning strategy can be one of the most rewarding aspects of trading. Creativity plays an important role in this process, and I find it refreshing to use a little creativity in a job that typically punishes the act of thinking too much.

The first step in becoming a glitch hunting trader is a radical readjustment in the way one views the markets. Any belief in efficient markets is renounced; likewise, dogma of technical and fundamental analysis, while not renounced, becomes more peripheral. Instead of time spent looking at fanciful technical patterns and thumping through earnings reports, the glitch hunter looks for the leaks in the market structure: arbitrage, inefficiencies, and repeating patterns. Glitch hunting in the financial markets requires plenty of time and patience, making it a quest suited for active/professional traders. Executing a glitch trade may only take a few seconds, but finding a glitch could take months or even years—the wait can be excruciating.

You need capital. You need time and patience. And you need access to decent trading hardware, software, and data feeds. Without a view of the inner workings and order flow of the market, the glitch hunter is flying blind. Access to market-depth data (Level 2 in stocks), auction data, and reliable and fast executions are imperative. Finding the tools that will help you unearth these glitches is part of the journey, because there are plenty of valuable resources out there depending on what market you trade.

After the necessary time and resources have been made available, the next step is finding these glitches. Observation and perseverance are the keys, so countless hours must be spent staring at market maker boxes, scouring charts for mysterious candle wicks, and examining different markets for potential arbitrage opportunities. This all must be approached with that hacker mindset, always looking for what is broken. Since there are thousands of instruments to trade, and the markets allow trading for the majority—if not all—of the day, it's best to focus on specific instruments, sectors, and time periods. Remember that volatile markets, sectors, or instruments provide a breeding ground for glitches.

It has gotten tougher with the proliferation of automated trading. Back when I started trading—before bots had taken over—the markets were teeming with glitches. Nowadays, these pesky bots have gotten deadly efficient at sniffing out opportunities and sucking the life out of them. To raise their odds of success, many traders join forces with the enemy and develop their own automated programs to hunt for and to execute glitch strategies. With or without the help of bots, the best traders keep improving their own tactics and can still make millions in today's market.

The trick is to be nimble and stay one step ahead of the trading bots. When you do discover a glitch, make sure you take full advantage of it because it will only be a matter of time before the enemy sniffs it out. It's a good idea to search for opportunities in markets that trading bots haven't completely infiltrated, such as the Cryptocurrency markets a few years back. These markets had pipes bursting everywhere and were fresh enough that they were relatively untouched by the bots, providing a perfect environment for skilled traders.

Let me make an important point here: If you are trading, you should be a "trader", rather than an "equity trader" or "futures trader". Don't limit yourself to one specific market or style, go to where the edge is. The greatest traders I know trade multiple markets and are always exploring for opportunities.

Another proven tactic in the battle against the trading bots is to attack while they are asleep. For the last five years, I have made the vast majority of my trading profits during the U.S. equity premarket and after-hours trading sessions. During these sessions that fall outside the official market open, the volume is a lot lighter because the main exchanges–the NYSE and Nasdaq–are closed, so trading is done on the smaller exchanges that have extended hours. Not only is the volume lighter during these sessions, but automated trading is also less prevalent, making these sessions fertile ground for glitch hunters and scalpers. The premarket session opens at 10 am European time, which is a good time to start the battle for us traders in Europe. This translates to anywhere between 1 am to 4 am in the U.S., so only the most dedicated and elite American traders roll out of bed to seize the ample opportunities that these premarkets offer. The rule for any professional trader–glitch hunters and non-glitch hunters alike–is to find the periods during the trading day that offer the most opportunity and take full advantage.

Regardless of what time of day you are trading, or what markets you are focused on, glitch strategies are the most efficient method for a trader to make money in the markets. It's not a hypothesis; it's backed up by data from nearly every other trader I know. Knowing that, you have two options: wait for that once-in-a-lifetime moment when someone gives you a winning lottery ticket, or set out on the extremely challenging quest to find one of these glitches for yourself.

5.
My First Trades:
A Trading Career on the Cards

Glitches not only appear in markets; they also pop up in everyday life. My Texan mom living in Essex was a glitch. Hearing someone speak with an unfamiliar Southern twang on the outskirts of London was the equivalent of spotting a mispriced order on a financial market; they both don't belong there. One definition of a glitch is that it is an inefficiency–and my mother trading the sunny skies of Austin for the gray of Grays seemed like an extremely inefficient thing to do.

Not many Americans move to Essex nowadays, and it was even rarer in the 1970s. I think it was a mistake that took her there. She accepted a job out of college and moved sight unseen, probably thinking her destination was London. If that's the case, she's not alone in being duped. Hundreds of thousands of travelers arrive at London Stansted Airport each year only to discover that they are 40 miles outside the capital, deep in the Essex countryside!

Mistake or not, mom quickly assimilated to her new surroundings. She married a nice Essex man, and they had three children: me, John, and my younger sister, Ruth. We all led a pretty normal life in suburban Essex for the next decade. It was nice and pleasant, if unremarkable. But, one day, all of a sudden, my parents decided to roll the dice.

Homesickness, years of bad weather, and the general bleakness of Essex took their toll on my mother. That–together with the promise of the "good life" in

America–made my parents' decision to move us all to America unsurprising. America has always been the land of opportunity, and we had a free pass to this promised land, so this doesn't sound like some wild and risky move, right? Well, let me describe the way this transatlantic move was executed.

The bold and somewhat crazy plan began with my parents quitting their secure and stable jobs and then selling our home and all of our belongings. My brother and sister and I were then taken out of school in the middle of the academic year, so we could all fly to California on one-way tickets. Once in California, we would hit the road and find a place to live. You have to understand that my parents didn't even know what city or state we would end up in–the general idea was just somewhere on the west coast so my dad could find a job in the shipping industry.

It was a huge gamble to quit good jobs, uproot a family, and move halfway across the world with no clear plan. However, my mom was from the land of oil wildcatting and Texas Hold'em, so she wasn't afraid of taking a risk now and again, as long as it was calculated. She was also self-confident and instinctively knew how to judge risk and reward, so we all had full confidence in her (and my dad's) decision. Again, she had the perfect DNA for a trader, because trading boils down to the same thing; finding and evaluating a trade with good risk/reward (edge), and then executing it confidently and effectively. I'm sure that her experience gave her confidence. She'd already undertaken one trans-Atlantic move without really knowing her end destination, and that turned out pretty well. Now she was just doing the same thing again, but moving the other way...

I arrived in Los Angeles in the summer of 1988 tinged with sadness from leaving my family and friends but brimming with excitement about the adventure ahead. L.A. had topped the list of possible places for us to settle as it had a big port, great weather, and my aunt lived there. It also had

Disneyland, Universal Studios, beautiful beaches, skateboarding, and houses with swimming pools, so my siblings and I were all desperate to stay. However, our parents were scared off by the high cost of living, so we bought a car, loaded it up with our few remaining possessions, and hit the road.

For the next few months, we were vagabonds; on the road searching the whole west coast for a place to call home, moving from one cheap motel to the next. It was tiring, but we had some amazing experiences: we were shaken and scared by an earthquake in San Francisco, collected pillowcases full of candy on our first American Halloween in Phoenix, and saw some of the most beautiful places in America from the window of a moving car. I have always enjoyed an adventure, and it was amazing to be doing all this while all the other kids were in school, but living out of a suitcase soon got old, and we all began to get restless.

We were into our third month on the road when it was announced, quite out of the blue, that our new hometown would be Austin, Texas. My mother's hometown had never been on the list, and crucially for my dad's career in the shipping industry, it is five hours from the coast. It seemed like a strange decision, but it was set in stone. The nomadic existence was over, and my dad, at the age of 42, would go back to school and find a new profession.

Once we arrived in Austin, my parents quickly rented a house for us, and we finally got back into school. It was quite a culture shock for me as the American public schools were very different from the strict catholic school I had attended in England. I was used to authoritative nuns running the joint, and nice polite little English boys and girls saying their pleases and thank-yous. American schools seemed wild and anarchic in comparison! I was shocked that the children had the audacity to talk back to the teachers. Where was the order? And where were the uniforms?

It goes without saying that I was constantly mocked by my classmates for my peculiar accent. These provincial American kids had never heard such a funny thing, and I was bombarded by questions about whether I knew the queen. I quickly exerted all my energy into trying to lose this accent as quickly as possible, so that I could blend into my new environment. I had a strong motivation for doing so because quirky traits aren't overly appreciated by 11-year-olds. However, I do miss having a cool English accent (though it's debatable if an Essex accent fits under the cool category). Fortunately, or maybe unfortunately, a very poor version of my original accent makes an appearance on my return trips to England and gives my family there a good laugh.

Losing the accent wasn't enough. I also needed to assimilate with these kids and learn their hobbies, which is what led me to discover the amazing world of baseball cards. This hobby was a way to make friends in my new school, but baseball card collecting also turned out to be an amazing primer for the world of trading. With a barrier of entry of a couple of bucks, an actual market structure, and glitches galore, card collecting provided a first-class education for a young prospective trader.

Let me explain the hobby of card collecting for those not versed. I will concentrate on baseball, but there were also football, basketball, and hockey cards. Baseball cards are about the size of playing cards and each features a separate professional player. When I was collecting, there were 3 or 4 companies producing sets of these cards, which could be bought in wrapped packs of about 15 cards.

Each card had value, which typically corresponded to the player's performance. So if a batter was hitting a lot of home runs and having a great season, his card would go up in value—and the opposite for poor performance. There were a few other variables that could affect the price of a card. Condition was important; if the card had any imperfections, such as worn corners or creases, the value would go down. Also, the first card issued for a player, their so-called rookie card, was always worth more.

The value of these cards was determined by a monthly magazine named Beckett. It was the Bible for the masses of us playground traders, featuring tables that assigned a current price for every card. I have fond memories of rushing to the local store on my bike each month, excited to get the latest issue of Beckett so I could meticulously calculate the value of my collection (or my portfolio, if you will) and revel in my success.

Since these cards had value, and there was a pricing mechanism for them (the Beckett), we can say there was a de facto market. However, instead of trading taking place on an exchange, the trading floors were in children's bedrooms, on school playgrounds, and in baseball card shops. The market participants were mostly children, but there were also adults drawn to the hobby, some of whom probably even made a decent profit as semi-competent "traders" taking advantage of youngsters with less knowledge or understanding of market economics.

As we covered earlier, the most efficient trading method is to look for inefficiencies in a market and then exploit them. In the baseball card market, the greatest inefficiency was people not knowing the value of their own stock. Therefore, the most efficient strategy for success involved taking advantage of these "low information traders".

I remember having quite a few friends who had extensive baseball card collections, yet were quite oblivious to the fortune they were sitting on. It goes without saying that many traders offered uneven trades to these kids and exploited their lack of awareness or engagement; these were the prepubescent baseball card versions of the bumbling rookie traders who entered mispriced orders. I'm proud to say that I tried to steer away from exploiting my friends and worked on developing more moral strategies instead.

The first of these involved a value investing approach, with the goal being to find cheap and undervalued cards. My first foray into fundamental analysis consisted of me watching hours of baseball games and trying to identify the next big star. Once my research was complete, and I had found the cream of the rookie crop, I would scoop up as many of these players' cards as my $5 weekly capital inflow (my allowance) would permit. I'm not sure what qualified me for this strategy since I was 12 years old and had only known the sport of baseball existed for just a few months. Not surprisingly, I didn't have much success. If I had, rather than collecting baseball cards, my skills would have been better put to use as a professional baseball scout or general manager.

My next strategy relied less on my baseball acumen and more on a glitch in the pricing model in this market. Financial exchanges offer pricing of financial instruments at least 5 full days a week; the baseball card exchange—which consisted of the Beckett magazine—was offering pricing once a month! A lot happens in a single month of a baseball season. For example, a player can have a hot streak and turn a dismal season into a monster one, so my goal was to buy and trade the cards of players who had improved their performance since the last Beckett was published. If a player's card was worth $2 in May, and then he subsequently went on a monster hot streak, the gods who controlled Beckett magazine might increase the value to $3 in the June issue. My goal was to collect as many of these cards at the $2 valuation right before the June issue was released. Sure, some collectors were savvy enough to pay attention to what was going on in the baseball world and realize that the $2 value was an abbreviation, but most of my "friends" weren't as plugged in as me.

Now, you might say that I was exploiting people, which I previously claimed I never did! And I stick by it. In this case, I wasn't preying on naivety and underpaying for the cards. I was giving my friends the current market value and not a dime less. Needless to say, this "lagging strategy" of mine worked out quite nicely for me.

Unfortunately for me and the other baseball card collectors of the late 1980s and early 1990s, our successes led to nothing more than paper profits. Baseball cards not only gave me some of my earliest lessons on trading, but they also provided me with a great introduction to economics—especially the laws of supply and demand. You see, the hobby began to boom in popularity, the market was flooded with cards, and prices consequently plummeted. Barely a teen, I was taught a painful lesson about market bubbles.

While baseball card collecting didn't fulfill my fantasies of becoming a teenage millionaire, it was the second step (after my wins and losses in Broadstairs) on my journey to becoming a professional trader. These cards introduced me to the concept of a market structure and provided experience in basic strategy development. In both the arcades of Broadstairs and the playgrounds of Austin, glitch strategies offered the path to riches—and that's the lesson that has stuck with me for the next 30-plus years and counting. I also learned about the idea of finding a way of taking advantage of a delay in pricing. This later became the basis for the strategy that would earn me my first paycheck as a stock trader, and many subsequent others.

For the first six months or so of my professional trading journey, I was lost. With no plan, no winning strategies, and no discipline, I was more of a bad high-stakes gambler than a trader. Instead of effectively executing a strategy with an edge, the known way to success in trading, I was instead looking for thrills. This quest led me to trade higher-value stocks because even small movements make big money. One of my favorite high-dollar, high-action stocks was 3M Corporation, or $MMM, because it was one of the handful of stocks that traded over $100.

I'm gonna stop right here to state the obvious: picking a trading style or stock based on the amount of thrill it gives you is never a good idea!

However, after watching $MMM for a while–and paying a few thousand dollars for the pleasure of doing so–I discovered a glitch that would salvage my trading career.

3M is a huge American conglomerate, and its fortunes generally ride with the tides of the markets. It is also a member of both the Dow Jones and S&P 500 indices, so it makes sense that it generally moves synchronously with these indices. As every trader should, I had a chart of the S&P index on my trading monitor, and my chart of my beloved $MMM was positioned right next to it. It didn't take me too long to realize the correlation between the indices and $MMM. Then I observed a slight lag; while $MMM did indeed generally move in the same direction as these indices, there was usually a slight delay before 3M caught up to them, not a one-month delay like in the baseball card world, but at least a second or two.

Nowadays, armies of trading bots are programmed to buy and sell the components of each index as these indices move up and down. Back then, during the infancy of automated trading, things were a lot more inefficient. The poor little bots seemed to be a little slow to buy or sell this $MMM as the market moved, and this slight lag enabled me to jump in front of them and quickly buy and sell $MMM based on the movement of the S&P index. I had finally made a breakthrough, and it didn't take me long to start cashing in on this simple but effective strategy I had stumbled upon.

The Execution for this edge ladened strategy was pretty straightforward, I would have my $MMM chart and my S&P chart side-by-side on my trading screen and then stare at them all day, looking for instances when $MMM was lagging behind the S&P. For instance, if the S&P index shot up all of a sudden, I would look to quickly buy $MMM before it made its move up, and when $MMM made this almost inevitable move up, I would look to scalp (cover my position quickly) for a typically small profit. Eat, sleep, buy, scalp, repeat. The keys to executing this strategy were concentration and a little speed, two things I possessed, even if I lacked experience. After a couple of expensive lessons, I also found that it was important to keep up with any news related to $MMM, because this could cause it to move independently to the S&P.

I have learned over the years that the simplest strategies typically provide the most edge, and with this uncomplicated strategy, I steadied the ship and was consistently making money. I had gone from not having one net positive month to having three in a row, and my confidence was brimming. A great thing about this strategy was that it became even more profitable when market volatility became elevated; bigger spikes and drops in the S&P allowed for bigger subsequent spikes in $MMM. Fortunately for me, one of these volatility spikes presented itself around my tenth month of trading, allowing me to have a $90,000 month! A few months prior, I would have thought a month like that was unimaginable. I was on cloud nine. I had passed the toughest test and received the most rewarding thing in the trading business: my first big paycheck.

It wasn't all smooth sailing after that; this $MMM strategy became less fruitful as the bots caught on. The lag gradually got smaller before eventually vanishing. Therefore, I had to get more resourceful and search for other similar lags in the market. With over 10,000 stocks and hundreds of sectors to choose from, I enviably found other opportunities that the bots hadn't yet devoured.

I have used this simple, but highly effective strategy in many variations over the years, including:

- Other stocks that have lagged the S&P index

- Stocks that lag their sector

- Sectors that lag the S&P

- Sectors that lag an underlying commodity

- Commodities that lag the S&P.

Other good examples would be trading an oil stock that lags the spot price of crude oil or a bank stock that lags the banking index.

A variation of this lagging strategy also brought me great success during the COVID market panic. In March 2020, the markets were going wild, and the S&P lost over 20% in a few weeks. Gold and gold mining stocks were especially volatile. Knowing from experience, and applying a little logic that gold mining stocks follow the price of gold, I was curious if there was any lag between the two. After simply comparing the charts of the price of gold and the prices of these gold mining stocks, my suspicions were confirmed, and I quickly dove in. It was as simple as trading gold stocks off the price of gold; if the price of gold spiked, I would quickly buy a lagging gold stock, and sell as soon as it caught up to the price of gold.

Another great thing about this strategy, unlike most others mentioned in this book, is that it can be used over a longer time horizon. The longer version of this strategy usually involves looking for a hot sector, such as marijuana stocks, and then searching for hidden or forgotten names that haven't made their move yet. I buy these in the hope they will be discovered and catch up with their brethren. Although I have had some luck with this longer-term version, my poor momentum trading skills typically let me down—even if I find a hot sector like marijuana, I typically get burned and cover my winners way before the biggest highs.

6.

American Schooling:
A Bettor Education

As a twelve-year-old, I felt totally euphoric opening a pack of baseball cards to find out if I had hit the jackpot and come upon a prized rookie card. I have experienced many other blissful highs since then, but the closest comparison is that dopamine hit I get when a casino dealer reveals the final card in my beloved game of blackjack. So after the baseball card market imploded, it's no shock that I eventually was drawn back into the world of gambling, only this time, my exploits ended up taking me to neon-lit Las Vegas, a world away from the flashing lights of a Broadstairs arcade.

At first, I stopped chasing riches and turned my attention to more traditional teenage pastimes. Soccer was always a passion of mine, and I guess you could say I discovered a glitch when I went from being a mediocre player in soccer-mad England to being somewhat of a soccer star in Texas. Unfortunately, this scale works both ways, as I went from having a good set of teeth in England, to having these same teeth being fit with thick metal braces in Texas. At least these braces helped me achieve my goal of looking like my peers and my newly adopted accent made me sound almost like them too. Next, it was time to complete my transition into becoming a Texan by getting a pickup truck.

After examining the gigantic parking lot of my high school, it seemed it was a rite of passage for any respectable middle-class Texas boy to get a pickup once they turned 16, or at least that's what I told my parents. After plenty of begging, we worked out a deal where my parents would buy me an affordable truck if I got a part-time job. So, I cleaned tables in a barbecue restaurant and graciously received an old Chevy pickup truck in exchange. This truck finally gave me the freedom I had dreamed of, I was 16 and could go wherever I wanted. Where did I go to take advantage of this newfound liberation? The horse racing track, of course.

Not only is it highly unusual for a 16-year-old to venture off to a horse track, but it's also highly illegal as the gambling age is 21 in Texas. Luckily for me, I was blessed with the most desired trait that an American male teenager could ask for; facial hair. The drinking age across the U.S. is also 21, so an immeasurable amount of time is spent by most American minors concocting plans on how to buy alcohol. It turns out the most successful strategy for buying alcohol as a minor is to grow the thickest beard you can, and then try and trick the most gullible, or profit-hungry, store worker into selling you alcohol.

My popularity definitely spiked with every successful alcohol purchase, but I was just as happy that this stubble of mine allowed me to get back to my roots, and back to betting on the horses. This time these were living, breathing horses, not the electronic ones from the arcade. The beard worked even better at the race track; while most liquor stores were on the lookout for courageous bearded minors, I was probably the only 16-year-old interested in placing a trifecta wager at a horse track.

My odds of being able to successfully place a wager were also boosted by the fact that this was no ordinary racing track, this was an extremely sketchy Quarter Horse track. No offense to Quarter Horses, but this is a big step below thoroughbred racing. Quarter horse racing appeals to only hardcore gamblers or hardcore equine lovers; I'll let you guess what category I fit in. These horses run sprints on tiny little tracks, with purses sometimes in the hundreds of dollars, making it the most unglamorous form of an otherwise glamorous sport.

This horse track sat on "the wrong side of town" and consisted of a couple of small dusty metal stands, a short racetrack, and a few wagering booths. Even though it was only about ten miles away, this dusty track felt like it was light years from the sheltered existence of my leafy upper-middle-class neighborhood of Austin. I'm sure I stuck out like a sore thumb as the rest of the sparse crowd was mostly middle-aged Mexican cowboy types.

I guess my suburban high school friends would have found the horse track to be a dreary and intimidating place, but to me it was exotic and intoxicating. However, I wasn't there for sightseeing and cultural exploration, I was there to make some cash. As you can imagine, I failed miserably. Handicapping horses is extremely tough, especially for a 16-year-old. When betting on horses, you are wagering that you are smarter than the rest of the gamblers—but these guys had all been around the block more than once.

I tried a variety of strategies at the track. The first incorporated a little fundamental and technical analysis, carefully studying the racing program for the horses' bloodlines or for any trends in recent races. After this strategy failed miserably, I moved on to less scientific methods like picking horses based on looks, name, or silk color. Unsurprisingly, those strategies weren't successful. In reality, I could have just gone with my tactic in the arcade at Broadstairs and bet on number two each time.

Fortunately, my losses were small—just as they were when I was ten—not because of any credence to the principles of risk management, but because I had little to lose. Regardless, these small losses were well worth it considering the cultural and life experiences these trips were providing. Despite the losses, the jaunts to this decrepit racetrack only whetted my appetite for the seductive world of gambling.

I wasn't a model student. I had this budding gambling habit, and I was highly unmotivated at school. I skipped my S.A.T. test (The U.S. college admission test, which has huge ramifications on the rest of your life) so I could go fishing. I figured it didn't matter, as I planned to attend the local community college once I graduated high school and focus on my true passions of partying, gambling, and fishing.

My plans changed when I was offered the opportunity to play American football at a major university in Texas. As you might have guessed from the beard, I matured quickly. I had the size, competitiveness, and athleticism to become a decent (American) football prospect, having swapped over from (English) football at high school. I didn't generate much interest scholarship-wise, but just before I enrolled at the local community college, Texas Tech University invited me to try out for the team. Texas Tech is a major college with a big-time football program, so I was flattered and immediately ditched my plans and headed to Lubbock, Texas.

I am fortunate enough to say that I have traveled the world, but Lubbock is still one of the most unique places I have ever visited. It sits in the middle of nowhere in the plains of West Texas (hundreds of miles from the closest city), stinks like shit (literally, there is a huge stockyard on the edge of town), there are dust storms (yes, like in the desert), and tumbleweeds blow through town (like in old Western movies). Strangely, these characteristics added to the city's character. Lubbock somehow also acquired a reputation as a party school–despite the fact that it was in a "dry county". The town sits in one of the most conservative areas of the U.S. Bible Belt and, just like in prohibition days, you couldn't buy alcohol within the city limits. That meant most students' Friday night ritual consisted of a drive out to the row of brightly-lit liquor stores called "The Strip", that sat just across the city line.

On my arrival in Lubbock, I quickly realized that I wouldn't be able to beat the long odds to become an elite college football player. Instead, I decided to focus on taking advantage of Lubbock's hard-earned reputation as a fun party town. After relinquishing my football dreams, I realized that to fully reach my potential and thrive in the upper echelons of the Lubbock partying scene, I would have to join a fraternity.

I'm happy to tell you that this is another area where my beard came in helpful. As strange as it may sound, a beard was a hot commodity when joining a fraternity. Other important things in this cliquish world included: wealth, family connections, good khaki trousers, popularity, and white skin color. It was an alien world to me, but I was willing to sacrifice some of my morals to be able to hang with the cool kids and the pretty girls drawn to this scene.

Possessing a beard, a firm handshake, nice khakis, and a couple of connections, I was able to receive an invite from one of the "top" fraternities. Why was it the top? Well, because they considered themselves the top. That confidence wasn't based upon academic pedigree or a commitment to wholesomeness, it was because they partied hard and had money (well at least their parents did).

The parking lot at our fraternity house looked like it was for the directors of a Fortune 500 corporation. These "brothers" of mine were living like kings! Our backgrounds definitely were different, but I did my best to fit in, bonding over cold beers and sports. It didn't take me long to discover that a sizable group of these guys also shared my passion for gambling.

Since we shared a love of gambling, I also thought it might be possible for them to share part of their sizable disposable incomes with me. My radical plan for wealth redistribution revolved around hosting blackjack games at my apartment. This did carry risks because, even though "the house" should always have the edge in blackjack over time, there is still the possibility that a player with a hot hand can wipe out the house. Considering I didn't have the money to pay out if there were big losses, it was indeed quite a risk; however, even at that age, I was aware of the amazing edge that casinos command, so I felt it was a risk worth taking. Fortunately, these guys started the nights as bad gamblers and became truly awful gamblers after a few beers, handing an ever-greater advantage to the house.

My casino night provided me with some much-needed spending money, but sadly, it didn't satisfy my gambling thirst. To parlay my blackjack winnings into some serious cash, I thought I needed to be on the other side of the table, placing the bets. Combining my two passions of sports and gambling always seemed a surefire way to quench this thirst of mine, but I never had access to this magical world. That's until one of my fraternity brothers graciously offered to introduce me to his bookie.

This bookie promised to unlock the gates to the world of sports gambling for me, but just as exciting, he was going to open the doors to the glamorous world of organized crime. I had heard all about bookies while watching my beloved mob documentaries, and I was hoping to get a glimpse into this dangerous world. However, suffice to say, a bookie who takes $20 bets off college students in Lubbock wasn't connected to the Gambino crime family. In fact, he was a 30-year-old living with his mom. Clearly, I wasn't gonna be a "made man" anytime soon!

Sports gambling is similar to betting on horses because you are basically betting against the other bettors. As you can imagine, if I was confident I was smarter than the other bettors at the horse track, then I was dead certain that

I was smarter than the other sports gamblers. I was an ex-football player, a certified sports junkie, and a walking sports encyclopedia.

In America, sports betting is usually done through a point spread, which is a number set by the oddsmakers to predict the margin of victory. The team you bet on has to 'cover' or beat that margin for you to win your bet. For example, if Texas Tech is 3-point favorite (a 3-point spread), then they have to win by more than 3-points for you to win your bet. If they are a 3-point underdog, they can't lose by more than 3.

I tried to avoid the most popular strategy, which is to just bet on your favorite teams to cover the point spread (I would compare the gamblers who rely on this lazy strategy to traders who rely solely on technical analysis). As tempting as this is, I took some initiative and attempted to develop my own more scientific strategies. At least I was on the right track because—as I learned later in the world of trading—carving your own niche is a path to success. Of course, that niche should have an edge and be executed efficiently, both of which were lacking in my gambling.

Fortunately, the losses were small, and I even had limited success with one strategy. This involved going through all the coming matchups without looking at the point spread, and instead deciding what I thought the point spread should be. I would then compare my point spread with the actual point spread and look for ones with a big variance. For example, If I thought Texas Tech should be a 10-point favorite, but they were actually a 1-point favorite, betting on Texas Tech would be the value bet for me. You could look at it as an offshoot of value investing, but I considered it a type of arbitrage, confident that I knew more than the professional oddsmakers in Vegas, and thus assumed their spreads were mispriced.

I definitely lost a little over those college years, which isn't so bad considering I enjoyed this pastime. All-in-all no harm was done, but my dreams of becoming a professional sports gambler had been dented. No worries though, I quickly found another avenue to quench my gambling thirst and provide me with the hope of riches: Las Vegas.

This opportunity arose when my college girlfriend graduated early and moved out to Los Angeles to attend graduate school. Lynsey–who obviously was quite a bit more motivated than me–was a great girl and an amazing catch for me. I had one year left of school, so we devised a plan where we would try to see each other regularly for the next year, and then I would join her in L.A once I graduated. By the time my senior year rolled around, I had mastered the art of getting by on attending the bare minimum of classes and studying as little as possible. I had chosen international business as my major, basically by default, and in return, this major proved immensely unstimulating and unchallenging. I'm sure a lot of the disinterest had to do with the quality of the business school. For example, it seemed strange that I didn't even need to take a foreign language course to complete my international business degree.

However, I was just happy that it was not a tough major and that it afforded the freedom to escape Lubbock occasionally to visit Lynsey in L.A. To make things even better, the U.S. government graciously offered to fund my getaways by approving me for a sizable student loan.

It was on my maiden visit to L.A that we made our first jaunt to Vegas. It was a spur-of-the-moment decision, which came with some risk, considering I was still technically too young to gamble. However, by this time my beard had become even thicker, and I had the added security blanket of having the old driver's license of an older friend who somewhat resembled me (we both had brown hair). Driving through the desert from L.A that first time, a feeling of exhilaration nearly caused me to drive off the road when I got a glimpse of the famous bright lights of Vegas in the distance. I was immediately hooked. The place was magical, the casino floors pulsated with energy and excitement, and the buzz I felt at those tables nearly knocked me out of my seat.

Blackjack was my game of choice. Although the house has the edge in this game, the player can slice that edge until it's razor thin if they stick to the rules of when to take cards and when not to, and weigh their bets properly. These are the same rules that apply to a successful trader; stick to your winning strategy and stay disciplined with your risk management. Staying disciplined is the key in both endeavors, which is always a challenge, and can be made even more challenging if you are being fed free alcohol in a boisterous casino.

Lynsey and I played the role of a married couple as part of our plan to appear that we were legitimately over 21. I surprisingly gambled like a responsible adult as well, staying disciplined and sticking to my strategy. Lo and behold, I won $1000!

Winning money anywhere is an amazing feeling, but winning money at a buzzing table in the middle of the gambling and party capital of the world, while having beautiful women deliver you free alcoholic drinks, is something else. As you can imagine, having to go back to school in Lubbock was the ultimate buzzkill.

My thousand-dollar win and my student loan funded regular trips out to L.A that year. On most trips, we would make a quick excursion to Vegas. I didn't always win, but out of necessity, I kept my losses small. On my visits to L.A when we didn't make it out to Vegas, I would placate my gambling itch by having Lynsey drop me off at the horse racing track on her way to school. The track in Santa Anita is truly amazing; it has top-class races against a backdrop of the spectacular San Gabriel Mountains. I'd spend a day milling around the racetrack, soaking up the atmosphere, surrounded by the motley crew of the weekday afternoon gamblers. These were my true brethren, not my fraternity brothers back in college.

That final year of college was a truly memorable one, and included the added bonus of me somehow graduating. I had incurred quite a bit of debt, and really didn't learn anything valuable at school, but the lessons I learned while dealing blackjack, betting on football, and visiting Vegas came in quite handy on my subsequent trading journey.

Of course, my education continued, with the casinos of Vegas and Macau helping themselves to a healthy chunk of my trading profits over the subsequent years. I only heeded the call to common sense and graduated from my "schooling" once it became a fiscal necessity. Unfortunately, it wasn't just the casinos that were cashing in on my stupidity; my friends also got in on the action. One of these friends, Jared, hit the jackpot in 2008 when I bet him $15,000 on the outcome of the U.S. election.

2008 was the year Obama-mania swept the nation, and as much as I liked him and the movement, the contrarian in me had me very skeptical about his chances of winning the upcoming election. With the polls firmly in Obama's favor, Jared realized it was great value to accept my $15,000 straight-up bet that Obama would lose. I looked at the bet as more of a hedge than anything—if Obama won, I would be happy, and if he lost, I would be $15k richer. Obama won, and I remember the pain of losing $15k more than anything else, and to make matters worse, one of the first things he did was raise my taxes!

This costly gambling education has taught me that the chances of being a profitable gambler are close to zero—even lower than the odds of becoming a successful trader. Generating a gambling strategy with edge is hard enough, but it's the exorbitant "commissions" that a gambler pays which really make it a fool's game. A sports bookie typically takes a 10% cut of all bets, and a horse track close to 15%. Although a casino isn't charging a commission per se, we all know that the game is rigged, and the odds are firmly stacked in their favor. Already at least 10% in the hole, the gambler's chances of being consistently successful are pretty much cut from slim to none. In the similarly challenging world of trading, we typically pay less than 1% in commissions, meaning the sports gambler pays over ten times more in commissions than a stock trader.

You could say I am comparing apples to oranges, but gambling and trading are ultimately both battles against the risk-reward paradigm: how much am I risking, what is my reward, and what is the chance of me winning? Therefore, the mantra in both professions is the same: acquire a strategy with an edge, and then execute it with discipline. My advice, again, is to acquire a strategy with an edge in trading or in gambling, by finding a glitch!

Just like in trading, gambling also offers plenty of glitches—and I am not just talking about slot machine malfunctions. However, glitch hunting in the gambling world can be considered a little more dangerous as many of these strategies ride the thin line between legality and illegality, and even if these strategies are legal, there are still some sketchy figures and shady organizations which "regulate" that world. What's more, the bots and algos are also getting in on the game; as if old-school casino pit bosses, crooked bookies, and gambling regulators weren't enough to worry about, now you have computer programs gobbling up the edge.

Despite all these threats, a few crafty gamblers still find a way to profit with the help of glitch strategies and other unconventional methods. A few savvy poker-playing friends of mine managed to make a killing in the early 2000s online poker boom. At the time, it seemed that everyone who had watched a few hours of Late Night Poker on TV was suddenly itching to get online to try and outsmart opponents at the virtual poker tables. Most of this new influx of players obviously only had a superficial understanding of the game, making them sitting ducks for any half-decent players.

A couple of my friends who were experienced players raked in hundreds of thousands of dollars, preying on these suckers. Just as with my blackjack-playing frat buddies, the most opportune time was when the bars closed, and these bad players returned home worse for wear. These poor souls would then log into their poker accounts and then hand over their money to the superior, sober players circling in cyberspace. The "great" thing about this strategy was that this poker craze was a worldwide thing, so you could play this "closing time" strategy in every time zone in the world.

Other gamblers use more traditional glitch strategies, such as courtsiding. This cunning strategy, which rides the thin line between legality and illegality, is a great example of a lagging strategy. Courtsiding is essentially the practice of taking advantage of a delay in a bookmaker's ability to update their odds. It involves someone watching an event live and placing a bet before the odds are changed online. Courtsiding usually happens at tennis matches, where the bettor quickly places bets after important points are won or lost in a race to beat the bookie updating their odds, and also racing to avoid detection by the authorities.

The safest of all glitch strategies is a good arbitrage strategy, which can be found by skilled gamblers (or well-programmed bots) on certain betting markets. Arbitrage betting takes advantage of price discrepancies between bookies or betting exchanges. An example would be betting on a team to both win and lose, but with different bookies who have different prices, allowing the bettor to profit regardless of the outcome. Unfortunately, bots are sucking the life out of this and pretty much every other golden glitch out there.

Since computer algorithms can't sit at a casino table, card counting is a glitch left solely to a few brave and intelligent humans. Card counting is an attempt by a gambler to cut the casino's, or house's edge by keeping a running tally of all high and low-valued cards seen by the player. If perfected, this skill can be highly lucrative, but of course, it is highly frowned upon by casinos, which don't take losing lightly.

Whether it's a card counting strategy or a closing auction strategy in trading, the goal is always to take advantage of a glitch. As you can see, the glitch hunter thinks and operates similarly, whether trading or gambling; however, I firmly believe that financial markets provide a much more fertile hunting ground than the sketchy world of gambling. The lower commissions, the almost unlimited supply of instruments to trade, and the ability to leverage easily give the trader a better chance to succeed than the gambler. Another huge advantage the trader has is that there are occasional bouts of extreme volatility in our business. As I already explained, these spikes in volatility typically coincide with accompanying spikes in the skilled trader's profits. The phenomenon of volatility doesn't really exist in gambling, or at least in the same sense.

While there are a handful of successful professional gamblers out there, the vast majority of gambling is done recreationally. We do it for the thrill; we want that heavenly shot of dopamine. It's kind of cruel that our bodies would fill our senses with such a pleasant feeling while we lose our hard-earned money playing a game rigged in the casino's favor. Though we know it's rigged, millions of us still flock to casinos, and most of us are usually able to have a somewhat healthy relationship with this vice, making it an accepted form of recreation when done responsibly.

This is where gambling and trading greatly differ. There is no such thing as recreational trading, and it should never be done for the thrill or to get a rush.

If you don't have an edge, you shouldn't be trading. I understand a trader new to the game will not have edge right off the bat, a grace period for training is granted, but if you are looking to gamble or for good times, head to Vegas, not a trading floor. A trader isn't sitting at a lively casino table drinking Mai Tai's; losing while glued to your computer and begging the markets for mercy is absolutely no fun. If "the house", or the markets, has the edge, stay away! Without strategies with an edge, and the confidence and discipline to execute these strategies, the trader is indeed gambling, not trading. Not coincidentally, all of the darkest periods of my trading career came when I was gambling, not trading.

I'm not saying there can't be a thrill involved in trading because I still get a buzz from it after 20 years. It makes sense since we have been biologically programmed to get that healthy dose of dopamine when we face danger or risk. The big danger is that we get addicted to these sensations and look to trading as a means to get our fix. The truest form of pleasure should come from the sense of satisfaction and accomplishment from executing one's winning trading plan and trading to the best of one's ability, not from going all-in at the flop.

Part II

A Trading Journey

7.

Starting Out as a Trader: Brokers and Broke Clients

You could say I found a glitch in the U.S college system. I was able to get a business degree from a supposedly respectable university in four years without really doing anything. I had spent my senior year gallivanting around California and Vegas, and the previous three academically disengaged. Surely, something must have been structurally broken? However, the integrity of the American educational system wasn't my main concern. I was more worried if this generic business degree would open the doors to a professional day trading career for me.

Yes, I had already been enticed by the world of day trading. These were the days of the original tech bubble (pre-pop); consequently, trading was enjoying one of its many renaissances. I had heard the dudes in this glamorous world sat in front of gigantic CRT monitors, bet on the stock market, and made tons of cash. It sounded even better than gambling, so I decided to conduct a little research during my senior year in between my jaunts to California and Vegas. This research consisted of me thumbing through the business pages of the newspaper, picking a few stocks from the tables, and then seeing if they went up or down in the subsequent days. It seemed I had the golden touch, as my picks only went up. What I didn't realize was that my "research" coincided with the internet boom, when the market was exploding and any company with a .com plastered to its name was going ballistic. I thought trading was almost too easy. All I needed was a decent amount of cash to get started in earnest—but that was something I didn't have.

Trading seemed like the perfect profession for me, but I did have one more option, which was to stay in school for a couple more years and get my teaching credentials to become a high school football coach. This was also a career that interested me, and the thought of a couple more years of living the good life in college also sounded appealing. However, I was gambling that Lynsey would accept me breaking our pact to live in L.A together after graduation. Unfortunately, I misplayed my hand, and she dumped me.

Although she was the most wonderful girl, I was too scared to follow through on our deal. I wasn't brave enough to move out of my comfort zone, so I chose to stay in college and go back to football coaching. However, this also fell to pieces, so it was back to chasing my trading dreams in the comfortable and familiar setting of Austin.

I'll admit that there was a mixture of heartbreak, embarrassment, and relief at having to move back in with my parents and live in my sister's old bedroom with its flowery wallpaper and four-poster bed. It didn't seem like a big step forward, but at least I had a base to jumpstart this trading career of mine.

Unfortunately, my Essex trading pedigree meant nothing in Texas, and learning the business at a street market would be impossible. The thought of starting my journey at a hedge fund appealed to me; I was definitely up for a high-powered job at a trading desk in the City of London or New York. My degree, college grades, and lack of connections quickly extinguished that dream.

Dirt broke and living with my parents, I was in no shape to trade my own funds, so a salaried job was needed, with the goal of finding some other poor sucker to fund my trading education. I stumbled upon a job listing for a junior stockbroker in my local newspaper. I was familiar with the movie "Wall Street", so the posting sounded exciting and dangerous. I thought being a stockbroker could also provide a great introduction to the world of finance since I assumed they spent their time studying the markets and providing hot stock picks–getting filthy rich in the process.

After a couple of shaky interviews, I somehow landed the job at Olde Discount Broker. It wasn't a high-powered hedge fund, and the name doesn't quite have the same ring as Goldman Sachs, but I was still proud of myself and excited to enter the world of high finance. I felt like a young Gordan Gecko, as long as I ignored the facts that I was waking up in my flowery wallpapered room, draped in a cheap and ill-fitting suit, driving a 10-year Nissan, and working in a sketchy strip mall in the Austin suburbs.

My first few months were spent studying for the dreaded Series 7 license exam. This is the license needed to flog securities to the public and is renowned for its extremely high failure rate. While diligently studying, I acclimated to the office and the stockbroker culture. The office was made up of six senior brokers and a few junior ones like myself–all male, of course. The senior brokers were characters straight out of the Wall Street movies; or at least that's what all their bling and swagger would suggest. It seemed the majority of their income was spent on cars, clothes, and watches. They also enjoyed frequent happy hours, late nights at the bar, and rounds of golf. This culture, and the banter associated with it, meant the atmosphere at the office was more like that of a locker room than a place of work; instead of the smell of locker room sweat, there was the scent of the whisky wafting from the mixed drinks sitting in styrofoam cups on the broker's desks. I was quite enthralled by all of it and tried my best to assimilate.

Having conquered the Series 7 exam and garnished with a registered financial representative license, I was congratulated by the firm with a gift of a colossal white phone book. The expectation was that I would call random numbers in this book, then impress and charm these unfortunate and unsuspecting strangers with my vast financial service expertise. Finally, I would try to close the deal by pitching them an underperforming mutual fund that happened to offer a nice fat commission.

This wasn't what I imagined stockbrokers did; I thought I'd be performing technical and fundamental analysis, and picking my favorite stocks for all of the firm's rich clients. I gave this cold calling a try for a few weeks and found it totally soul-destroying. My masters taught me that it was best to prey on old people who were lonely and looking for someone to talk to, or on rich housewives while their husbands were away at work. I didn't want any part of this. Even though this was technically what I was being paid to do, I gave up even trying after a month.

The payment for all of this devious sales work was a base salary of $2,000 a month. After a year, the salary would be cut, and the pay would become commission based, meaning I would HAVE to sell. I was enjoying collecting the $2k a month, and the extracurricular activities like happy hours and golf, so I came up with a cunning plan, or maybe what you could even call a glitch strategy: skate by for the rest of my first year without doing any cold calling, collecting my monthly salary, and then quit on my one-year anniversary.

I kept busy the majority of the time by doing office chores. My coworkers bestowed on me the nickname "Chim Chim the Monkey", and my lovely boss would shout out "Chim Chim!" to alert me that his coffee needed refilling. My other duties included filing, running errands, and calling existing clients about account issues. Account issues in the year 2000 usually meant margin calls. The dot-com madness was over, and many investors had arrived late to the party and were leveraged to the hilt; so, when the bubble finally popped, things got ugly. My job was to call these unfortunate investors and inform them that they needed to come up with cash—usually within hours or even minutes—or the firm would sell a chunk of their assets. Dealing with these sometimes irate or grief-stricken clients wasn't fun, but it still beat cold calling.

As busy as these margin calls kept me, I wasn't able to totally evade these dreaded cold calls, so I kept the senior brokers off my back by faking these calls. These "ghost" cold calls consisted of me dialing a number that didn't exist and then having an imaginary conversation in earshot of a senior broker. Even with a 0% conversion rate on my cold calling, my plan worked (I guess with the market getting pounded, it made sense I wasn't getting too many bites pitching stocks to strangers), and I collected my monthly $2,000 for the rest of that first year.

I was happy to exit the brokerage world. I didn't look at it as a failure because I learned a lot. I found out that the world of stockbrokers—especially sketchy discount brokers—is murky and unscrupulous. These brokers would do or say anything for a sale, flogging whatever would pocket them the biggest commission, regardless of suitability or performance. Although the word "stock" figured prominently in their job description, their lack of knowledge about the markets was truly shocking. I was flabbergasted that brokers who managed hundreds of millions of dollars lacked even the most basic understanding of how the markets worked. Yes, Olde was definitely one of the more shady outfits, but I have heard plenty of stories involving other more "prestigious" brokers. I assume, or at least hope, that there are good brokers out there. Regardless, my experiences have taught me to be suspicious of this industry, and the world of finance in general. Sadly, the subsequent 20-plus years spent as a professional trader has done little to alleviate these suspicions.

Although my experience left a bitter taste about the business of finance, my interest in the markets was only sweetened. Every opportunity given to evade the prying eyes of the senior brokers at that office was spent combing through research reports and gawking at the live stock quotes available on those primitive computer systems. I compiled mock portfolios, paper traded my favorite stocks, and learned basic technical analysis. Thankfully, the trading was just on paper because things were ugly, the markets were in a nosedive. I had begun my long-term relationship with the markets at a traumatic time; the Nasdaq lost 50% in my one year as a broker!

This was my introduction to volatility, and the destruction this phenomenon can deliver.

Not having any skin in the game meant I was immune from the devastation, and it was quite exhilarating watching these monster waves of volatility hit. I was in awe of the destruction they caused, but also became aware of the tremendous opportunities they provide to skilled investors, traders, and bottom pickers.

Personally unscathed from the market carnage and ready to conquer the world of trading, I quit my job at Olde on my one-year anniversary. My ever-present gambling habit had meant I wasn't able to save much of my salary, and only the equivalent of one month's pay made it to my savings account. Confident that this $2000 was enough capital to start a professional trading career, convinced that my year as a broker was adequate training for a new profession, and certain the market was bottoming, I eagerly opened a trading account with an online broker.

Working from my parent's computer with its super-slow dial-up internet provided a challenge. Trading without a plan—as well as no strategies, no risk management, no training, little capital, and an inclination for bottom picking—proved an even bigger challenge. Within a week, my money was gone, and my dreams of being a trader were vanquished.

To be honest, I have no recollection of what, or how I traded, I just knew it was all over before I knew what hit me. Considering how ill-prepared I was, it was only going to be a matter of time before I got wiped out, especially in such a turbulent market. It's surprising that I even lasted a week!

Sadly, I didn't really learn many insights about the actual trading process from this brief adventure; it was all a blur. But at least I learned how tough this industry was and how unmerciful the markets can be. I now knew that I needed support and guidance to succeed, and that I couldn't attempt this mission alone. In hindsight, I was lucky to only have $2,000 at my disposal; if I'd had $50,000, I am certain I would have lost that. The same odds of success (0%) apply to any new trader attempting to jump into the markets as I did.

I really can't emphasize this enough. It's the most valuable thing I can tell any aspiring trader. Don't start out without the proper support and guidance! Surrounding oneself with experienced and successful traders is the best—perhaps the only—way to have a fighting chance in this brutal game.

Battered but not beaten, I longed to get back into trading. Without a direct path, it was necessary to find another job to support myself. Taking a job as a caddy at a local golf course was hardly a bold career move, but it was something to tide me over. Carrying heavy golf bags around a hilly golf course in the 100-degree heat of a Texas summer quickly cleared my head. I was even more determined to make my dreams come true and become a professional trader. Re-energized, I managed to find a firm in Austin that was hiring and seemed to be the exact type of company I was looking for. None of this cold calling and client nonsense, this was a proper trading company; a proprietary trading firm (a prop firm), the type that funded traders to trade independently, trained them, and then took a split of the profits in return. It seemed too good to be true!

Part of the requirements for this job was a Series 7 license, so I had at least something going for me, and it was enough to get me in the door for an interview. Walking through doors emblazoned with Zone Trading in big letters, I knew I had found my home. The trading floor had testosterone hanging like a fog over the rows of gigantic old-school monitors. Screams of "Fuck you!" and "You piece of shit!" filled the air as a room full of young guys clad in Hawaiian shirts, shorts, and flip-flops pounded on keyboards. I noticed half of these screams were coming from guys who weren't even trading; they were playing shoot-em-up video games. It seemed blowing someone's head off in a video game and pulverizing a keyboard was the preferred method to let off a little steam between bouts of trading. The whole scene was quite euphoric—and the shots of vodka I took to calm my nerves for the interview only added to the buzz.

I joined a trading manager in a side office for an interview, and—in between the constant interruptions of traders barging into the office and asking for "more size", which seemed a peculiar request at the time—I was told tales of traders making tens of thousands of dollars in a single month. Knowing what I know now, and considering how easier trading was back then, tens of thousands seems ridiculously unimpressive. Those traders, trading in markets teeming with glitches, should have been making millions! Of course, at the time, I was in awe. Luckily, the office manager didn't smell the alcohol on my breath during the interview—or maybe he did and marked it as a plus, assuming I wasn't afraid of taking risks.

My Series 7 license was truly a saving grace. The fact that I already had it would save the firm from having to pay for me, or more likely, another recruit, to take this exam. After a couple of days of nervously waiting, I got a call saying that I had gotten the job. My parents weren't quite as thrilled as me when I told them the job offered no salary and had a 95% failure rate. Moreover, if I did succeed, it would take at least a year or two to see the real rewards. However, I had little doubt that I would succeed, and one more year of living with my parents, and working a side job in the evenings, was a small sacrifice for me to have my dream job. And it wouldn't matter in a year when I was filthy rich.

8.

A World of Volatility and Change: Taking Scalps

My new coworkers called him The Zuck. It wasn't because of the fact that every other word out his mouth rhymed with "zuck", and it was a few years before the other guy in the hoodie hit the scene. It was just a shortened version of his surname, Zuckerman. My new boss was straight old school; a foul-mouthed, flat-topped Jersey guy, the size of a house, who had sharpened his teeth—or rather fangs—trading in the pits of the Mercantile Exchange. He wasn't a pat-you-on-the-back type of guy; he was more a bite-your-head-off boss. It wasn't unusual for a trader to escape his office following one of his "trading evaluations" in floods of tears. I will never forget my introduction to The Zuck; on my first day at the office, I gave him a friendly look and smile as he emerged from his office, and he blasted out, "What the fuck are you looking at?!"

Unsurprisingly, The Zuck wasn't into elaborate and structured training programs. I had expected that I would have months of meticulous classroom education ahead at this new job of mine; instead, I was handed a software manual and a computer and told to get going. I would have two weeks trading on simulation, and then I would go live, trading real money.

Talk on the testosterone-laced trading floor revolved around "killing it", trading "big size", and "making G's". Therefore, after graduating from my "training program" and being handed live ammunition, I transformed into the trading version of Rambo. Not knowing any better or having anyone to teach me anything, I went crazy. I traded like a wild man and used that live ammo to mainly shoot myself in the foot.

The pain couldn't have been too bad because I kept my finger on the trigger—even finding a glitch to allow me to trade "more size" and, therefore, cause more damage. Although I was only allowed to trade 100 shares of each individual stock, for some strange reason, I wasn't limited to the number of different stocks I could trade. So while I couldn't trade 200 shares in a single stock, I could trade 100 shares in 20 different stocks at a time. With this trick up my sleeve, it took me little time to master the impressive act of losing thousands in a single day.

My wild approach and the boisterous atmosphere made the trading floor feel more like a casino floor—and since I was playing with the house's money, the losses didn't sting that much. The problem was that I wasn't the disciplined blackjack player in this casino, I was the fool going for broke on the roulette table. It would probably have been best for The Zuck to act like a "pit boss" and cut my limits, or at least kick me up the ass. However, I escaped his wrath and the only punishment I received was courtesy of the markets, which at this time were even more temperamental than my boss.

The markets were wild. The dot.com bubble had burst, and investors were further spooked when Enron blew up. Enron was an energy company that was the darling of investors until its accounting books turned out to be fraudulent, further eroding investor confidence. Things seemed like they couldn't get worse...

During my second month on the job, I walked into the office and saw the shocking images of smoke billowing from the First World Trade Center. While most of us stared at the TVs with our jaws dropping, many of the veterans sat glued to their computer monitors with their fingers pumping. I was too naive–and too shocked–to realize that this was exactly the kind of event that creates the market volatility that a trader thrives on.

Those "savvy" veteran traders didn't have too much time to trade because it was promptly announced that the markets would be closed indefinitely. After a week or so off–and after letting all this horrific news sink in–it was announced the markets would reopen, and we went back to work. Although we were seldom given guidance from the senior traders, I do remember that on this occasion, one of our more respected colleagues stood up in front of the whole office and gave an impassioned speech right before the markets reopened.

He told us that it was his patriotic duty that day only to buy stocks; he was not going to short and he encouraged the rest of us to follow his noble lead. I respected his morality and wondered how many of his fellow senior traders would get on board. It turned out that few followed, and the ones that did paid dearly because the markets got hammered. It's another excellent example of how morality and trading don't mix.

The markets eventually steadied, but my P&L did nothing but hemorrhage. I was lost, and without any type of meaningful trading plan and the mindset of a gambler, I managed to achieve the remarkable feat of losing almost $40k in less than five months. The fact that my secondary evening job was as a door guy at a nightclub didn't help matters. As soon as I left the trading floor, I would head home, take a quick nap, and then typically work at the bar till at least 1 am before having to be at the office by 7:30 AM. While working the door, my bartender buddy would offer me free and irresistible, ice-cold beers, offering a stern test for my sense of discipline. It turns out my discipline was even laxer at my night job than at my day gig.

The environment at the office felt even more chaotic than at the nightclub. Not only did we have a crazed boss and no training program, but midway through my first year at the office, a good chunk of the firm's most profitable traders decided to leave and start their own outfit. This business naturally has high turnover, I've seen thousands of traders come and go over my career, making me feel somewhat like a death row inmate, not wanting to get too friendly to the guy next to me, knowing that it's only a matter of time till that seat lay cold and empty. Fortunately for these traders, and unfortunately for the firm, they weren't being led to the electric chair, instead they were escaping the madhouse for far better compensation. I just wished that I could have gone with them and relieved myself of the $40k debt hanging over my shoulders. Unsurprisingly, the invite never came.

After the renegades jumped ship, things seemed pretty bleak. Fortunately, this upheaval forced the owner, Andy Kershner, to make some needed changes. Out went The Zuck, Andy stepped up his involvement, and in came a more professional and forward-thinking management group. A proper training program was introduced, and a spirit of cooperation and friendly competition was encouraged to foster a productive environment to spawn some new profitable traders. To complete the transformation, the firm dropped its generic "Zone Trading" title and was renamed Kershner Trading.

Andy and the new management appreciated just how important a role the overall environment is for each individual trader's chances of success. It's necessary for a rookie trader to be surrounded by experienced and successful peers—even if these successful traders aren't kind enough to share their winning strategies or provide any type of mentorship or coaching. Success finds a way to seep from trader to trader, like some type of benevolent virus. Surrounded by winners, the confident trader has the attitude that if others can do it, they surely can too. This mindset is mandatory in a job where a fellow co-worker raises the white flag or is shown the door every week. It's no surprise that with this ceaseless body count, the trader needs constant reminding and reassurance that it is, indeed, possible to succeed.

Many of the traders who left in the purge had been using the rather malevolent "rookie sniping strategy," so many of us were actually glad to see the back of them. Regardless, the stock of elite traders needed to be replenished—either by bringing people in or elevating those on board to that level. My new bosses understood that healthy competition is a more effective motivator than verbal abuse, so they started rewarding the top traders in each category with a cash prize and other goodies each month. Management did a fantastic job of promoting these intensely competitive contests, strategically placing computer monitors (or, rather, let's call them scoreboards) throughout the office displaying every trader's profits (or, rather, let's be honest and say that, at the time, most of us had losses).

The size of my losses, and the embarrassment of having them broadcast across the office, should have been enough motivation for me to get my act in order, but competing in these competitions definitely added a little fuel to my fire. I was probably more focused on beating the other rookies and winning dinner at a fancy restaurant than the real prize of keeping my job and my trading dream alive.

The management clearly knew that trading is, by nature, a competitive sport. With a slim chance of survival, trading naturally attracts a group of ultra-competitive combatants. In fact, most trading floors at prop firms are filled with ex-athletes, gamers, and poker pros. Add in an extreme amount of testosterone, and you start to understand why some of these trading offices more closely resemble gladiatorial arenas than professional work environments. To compound the competitive element, traders at the office were divided into teams, and appointed a senior trader as a coach.

This program was a step in the right direction and the new structure gave new life and hope to my trading. Ultimately, it was still on my shoulders to turn things around. In spite of my continued losses, I still had the all-important confidence that I would make it. That was key because without confidence a trader is a dead man walking. So that's why I came up with a cunning plan, and the first step of this plan was to stop the bleeding. I had been trading like a wild man, intoxicated by the rush of big swings in my P&L (although saying "swings" is putting it kindly, as it was more of a downward spiral). I had been reckless and had ignored the most important lessons any new trader should learn and abide by:

CUT YOUR LOSSES

and KEEP THEM AS SMALL AS POSSIBLE!

Let me emphasize the importance of these words for all traders, especially newcomers. Rookies are clueless, losses are inevitable, so the number one priority for a new trader is to keep those losses tight and get their trading education as quickly and cheaply as possible. Cutting losses quickly will not only reduce the financial hole that a newbie will no doubt dig themselves into at the start; but even more importantly, it teaches discipline, which is a prerequisite for any successful trader.

I will begrudgingly accept that an experienced trader who is consistently profitable has earned the right to widen those stop losses, but a new trader has no such privileges and must keep those inevitable early losses as small as possible. Loose risk management is the number one cause of budding trading careers going up in smoke. Placing automatic stop-loss orders is the easy solution to this problem. So, here's the most important lesson for the first year of trading: Keep your losses as small as possible and get in the healthy and necessary habit of punching out of losing trades!

When I made the switch from being completely reckless to adhering to risk management principles, I was suddenly relieved by not having to constantly deal with the mental anguish that accompanies big losing trades. My P&L improved and my confidence grew. This newfound dedication to cutting my losses also led me to discover the ultra-fast trading world of scalping, which has been my home ever since.

Before diving more into scalping, let me first quickly categorize the different trading styles. For simplicity's sake, I will put them into two groups.

Scalping describes a style of trading in which trades are held for seconds, minutes, or, in some cases, hours. The skilled scalper takes profits quickly and covers losing trades even more quickly.

Position Trading (as well as Swing Trading) revolves around holding positions for hours, days, weeks, months, and maybe even years. The position trader relies on technical and fundamental analysis and hopes to ride the momentum of the markets.

You could say I started my trading career as a position trader. My initial trading strategy consisted of buying a stock, or basket of stocks, and hoping the market would show me mercy. If the market was unmerciful, which it tended to be, I would typically hold my position until my daily loss limit was met, and I was forced to cover. My reason for entering one of these "wing and a prayer trades" was typically some exotic technical pattern, maybe a "bullish pennant" or a "cup and handle pattern". I might occasionally hit a home run, but the vast majority of my trades were strikeouts. I was basically using the same strategy that 90% of the traders on Twitter use, and despite their bluster, I'm almost certain they suffer the same results.

Scalping is different; it's more about reacting than hoping. The skilled scalper is still technically at the mercy of the markets, but is constantly adapting to the dynamic situation, staying nimble and not attaching themselves to one side of the market. A scalper realizes that even though a trade setup might look perfect, the markets might not want to cooperate, and there is no point in fighting the markets. The trick is to look for warnings that the market is kind enough to share and act accordingly.

A warning could be a big seller in the order book, breaking news, or a sudden nosedive in the broad market. For example, it might look like the perfect long position, but if a huge seller pops into the order book, the skilled scalper will use their tape reading skills and quickly cover their position and look for the next opportunity—which may even mean switching sides and shorting that same stock in front of the big seller.

Scalping revolves around agility and speed, making it more like video gaming, but discipline is the most essential trait for any successful scalper. Cutting and keeping your losers as small as possible becomes paramount when your winners aren't as big. Although home runs are possible, the scalper aims to hit singles and doubles. These winning trades don't have to be huge, just bigger than the losers. If a trader (any trader) can follow this mantra, he or she doesn't even need to be right most of the time—even in my best months, my win rate typically hovers around 50%.

It all makes perfect sense to me, and that's why I have always resisted the temptation to switch sides and become a position trader. I don't want to go to bed knowing that some random geopolitical event overnight in Asia could destroy my trading account; scalpers sleep like babies. Why would I leave myself to the whims of the market? The position trader speculates by thinking or hoping that a stock will go up—and that sounds like gambling to me.

I say "gambling" partly tongue in cheek because I know successful position traders, and certain position trades offer plenty of edge, such as that $LVS trade I spoke about earlier. But ultimately, for me, it makes sense to scalp. Why not use these amazing tools available, such as order books, and why not operate mechanically instead of being totally exposed to the unpredictability of the markets?

My conversion to scalping helped slow my losses to a trickle, but I still needed some winners–and they were proving hard to find. Winning trades require good strategies, but mine were all duds.

It was tough extracting actionable information from the few profitable traders, but I still remembered how the group of traders who recently left had operated. How could I forget? I still had emotional and financial scars from the times they had picked off erroneous orders of mine. They fed on errors and arbitrage, looking for "free" cash. While I wasn't about to torpedo my colleagues, I did realize that I needed to adopt their approach and take advantage of the opportunities presented. I needed to find glitches.

Inefficient markets are the perfect place to look for such strategies, and even my semi-trained eyes were able to see that the stock market was not functioning perfectly. The early 2000s were a time of seismic changes in the stock market structure. The old-school NYSE market specialists, who strutted around on the stock exchange floor like creatures of an ancient era, were fighting a losing battle to protect their turf from a batch of new and competing electronic exchanges.

These electronic exchanges pathed the way for the second wave of attack, a full-on invasion by automated trading bots. The battle was intense, and the transition from the traditional market structure to the electronic market structure was messy, presenting countless opportunities for skilled glitch hunters. The regulators also contributed to the ripe pickings, bringing in new rules and regulations to tackle the problems and issues brought on by these changes in the market structure. Unfortunately for them—and fortunately for traders—many new rules and regulations just added to the chaos. I won't get too technical here, but I highly recommend reading *Dark Pools*, by Scott Patterson, for more background on this tumultuous time in the markets.

Now that I had narrowed my focus to these inefficiencies and glitches in the market, the next step was to find a specific glitch and take advantage of it. The problem was that most glitch strategies relied on speed, and I've always been pretty darn slow on the keyboard. I knew my odds were going to be better if I found a strategy that was less reliant on speed and had fewer vultures fighting for the scraps.

Automated trading had been around for a while by 2001, but the trading bots weren't the ruthless cash-printing monsters that they are today. Nowadays, stealthy bots have mastered the game of entering and exiting the market with as little detection as possible, but they didn't use to do such a good job of hiding their hand. Even with very little successful trading under my belt, I found that I could spot some of these clunky bots at work. For instance, they would always use the same electronic exchange and always display the same order size, and often chase the bid or offer of the stock they were attempting to buy or sell.

I was able to start to take advantage of some of these bots, eventually perfecting my lagging 3M ($MMM) trade that I mentioned earlier and ate away at my debts. My meteoric progress and the gaming aspects of these strategies gave it the feel of my younger days when I would use a cheat code to advance in my favorite video game. In fact, glitches ARE the trader's version of cheat codes! My new "cheat code" had transformed me into a turbocharged Pacman, only I was gobbling up cash, not pixels.

I was finally getting ahead of the market that had beaten me so badly for so long, applying a little discipline and finding a winning strategy had made all the difference. I felt on top of the world, and my confidence grew. After a $10,000-month in June 2002, I was only a few thousand dollars away from covering my losses and receiving that monumental first paycheck I had dreamed of.

In July 2002, I crossed that line into profitability in style, pushed by a huge wave of volatility that had laden my $MMM strategy with what I previously thought were unattainable profits. I finished that July with $90,000 in profits! Not bad for a 22-year-old playing a glorified video game.

9.

A Survival Guide for a Brutal Career:

Serious Advice for Traders

I swore I would never be the type of guy who complains about paying a bunch of taxes, hoping instead to look at it as an honor bestowed for success. However, when I saw how much of a cut both my firm and the government had taken from my first paycheck—chopping it down from high five figures to a paltry four—I immediately started griping. In fact, my swagger took just as much of a hit as my income did, as I was forced to take mommy and daddy with me to the car dealership to cosign for the brand new SUV I had just treated myself to because I could no longer secure the loan!

Buying a truck before getting paid felt like a superstar move—the type of thing that young athletes or entertainers do. I had beaten the odds and become a professional trader, making tens of thousands of dollars a month; I felt like a rockstar. I now even had the car to prove my status (just as long as nobody asked to see my flashy apartment and found out that I was still sleeping in a princess-themed bedroom at my parents' place).

To avoid this potentially embarrassing situation, I moved out into my own place after a few profitable months and was now officially free, independent, and self-reliant. Having reached that point, it was time to set new goals.

Goals for a successful trader typically revolve around making as much cash as possible—and then making more than your peers. The competition on the trading floor between the burgeoning group of successful traders kept us all focused. Not only did I want to be one of the top traders in the office, but I had also become a coach and wanted to lead the most feared team in the office.

The requirements for becoming a coach obviously weren't that stringent. It was pretty remarkable that I was leading a team of rookies considering the shape of my trading just six months prior. However, with few experienced traders to choose from, I was the next best thing.

Regardless of how I got there, I was excited to share with others the benefit of my recent and brief success. I still love this part of the job because trading is typically a very lonely endeavor, with results resting squarely on the shoulders of the individual trader. It's refreshing anytime you can work alongside others. I have found that teamwork eases the burden, usually making work more enjoyable and raising each trader's performance. Golf and tennis are similar to trading, in that results rest on the individual's performance, and I feel like these athletes perform better—or at least seem to have a lot more fun—when they participate in rare team events such as the Davis Cup or Ryder Cups.

Building the top team in the office meant recruiting the best prospects. Management shared my belief that being a good trader at least partly relied on genetics, so nepotism wasn't frowned upon. I brought in my ultra-competitive, non-risk-averse, bottom-picking brother, John. I figured he would be a good trader, but I also hoped that the life-long competition between us would bring out the best in both him and me.

Ryan was an old friend who was working as a golf pro. I knew that a competitive background is beneficial in trading, and Ryan takes things to a whole other level. He's the type of guy who can make playing a board game miserable! Even though he knew nothing about trading, I knew with that type of nature and with a good head on his shoulders he had a decent shot at becoming a successful trader. Sadly in this business, a "decent" shot at making it is as good as one's chances get.

The team was rounded out by one of my favorite traders of all time, Jeremy Liu. He was a gunslinger; the guy never saw a trade he didn't like and always begged for "more size". It was hard not to smile hearing him scream out, "I just lost a month's salary!" in his thick accent. Jeremy had a legitimate side job—something like a management position at a software company—but he bet so big on the markets that usually all those hours of work went to waste with a couple of keyboard strokes.

Plenty of other friends and acquaintances talked about getting in the game, undoubtedly enticed by the lure of easy riches. People see a 22-year-old friend making extravagant purchases and earning as much in some weeks as they do in a year, and everyone suddenly wants to try their hand at trading. This especially occurs during the good times for trading. In 2020/2021, the markets went wild, and everybody wanted to be a trader again—but I don't remember people begging to get into the business in the years before when the markets were calm, and I was dead broke.

Trading is not easy money. Prospering in this business takes a lot of hard work and skill. The markets will show no compassion for those who jump into trading unprepared and without the required passion. If your heart and soul aren't in it, and you haven't done your homework, then don't do it!

I don't discourage everyone from becoming a trader. Sometimes I will even try to get a friend to give trading a shot if I think they have the necessary traits to potentially make it.

Competitiveness is one of these traits. John and Ryan are both ultra-competitive, as was our friend Mike, who joined the trading crew a couple of years later. Mike and I had a history of epic Madden video game battles, and I had also known him to be a shrewd baseball card collector back in the day, so I thought he had the perfect resume for a trader. Mike, John, and Ryan are still making their living as professional traders almost 20 years later, so it seems I was on to something.

My good buddy Nate didn't have the key traits that make a trader. He and I both knew it wasn't the best fit for him—especially as he was quite risk-averse—but he wanted to give it a shot anyway. I envisioned the team I was coaching as more of a fraternity than a group of professionals, so he joined us even though I had little hope of him succeeding.

He was smart enough to pick the brains of the top traders in the office, and he stuck with it. When the 2008 craziness hit, Nate was fortunate to be sitting in that Austin office surrounded by some amazing traders and was kindly gifted that amazing glitch strategy. He stepped up and took advantage of this almost once-in-a-lifetime opportunity, making some nice profits—and then smartly exited the business once things started to get tougher. Not only is this another great example of the "power of the glitch", but I'd say that Nate's story highlights another necessary trait: he had the courage to take advantage of the opportunity that came along. Moreover, it takes courage and smarts to walk away when the time is right.

John and Ryan showed potential from the start, making steady progress in their first year, even at a difficult time in the markets. There was little volatility in the markets, and my own trading stalled. The six-digit paychecks I had expected did not materialize, though I was still bringing in more than enough to cover my basic needs, as well as a decent surplus for travel and fun.

My trading might not have been evolving, but the rest of my life was changing fast. My new girlfriend, Margaret, perhaps wasn't the perfect match for me, but she had a cute smile and a good sense of humor, and she was a ready and willing companion for sushi dinners and weekend getaways. Within a couple of years of dating, we were in the process of building our, or more accurately, my, dream house.

This came about when I discovered a prime piece of land for sale that sat above my boyhood fishing spot–the very place where I had skipped my college entry exam. I snapped up the land and fulfilled a fantasy by designing my dream house. The fact that the house was a glorified bachelor pad–complete with bars, pool tables, and fish tanks in the wall–was probably a strong sign to Margaret that I wasn't as ready to settle down as I was making out!

At 25, I had my dream job, my dream car, my dream house, and a nice girlfriend. I had accomplished a big chunk of my life goals (at least the material ones) at an early age, and was feeling quite proud of myself.

Obviously, it was time for things to fall apart.

The first crack–or rather black hole–in this perfect life appeared when my mother had a relapse of breast cancer. My family had been overjoyed just a couple of years earlier when we believed my mom had beaten this dreaded disease; but we knew that when cancer returns, it returns with a frightening vengeance. My mom was an extremely strong woman, but you could tell she knew she was in trouble, and it didn't take long for the toxic chemotherapy to transform a strong, beautiful, and spirited woman into a shadow of her former self. My mom was a fighter, but it was a battle she couldn't win. Watching her suffer and seeing her body get devoured by this cruel disease was the most painful experience of my life. Our family felt the pain at many levels. She was our leader and our captain, and her passing left us rudderless.

I thought a good way to deal with my grief would be to start a family of my own. Like myself, I don't think that Margaret genuinely felt like we were a perfect couple, but her friends were settling down, and she made it clear she wanted to get married. We could paper over the cracks with a big ring and an elaborate wedding.

It's rarely a great sign when you propose in Las Vegas, still drunk from the night before. However, she accepted, and now I had to tackle both an upcoming wedding that didn't quite feel right and the grief of losing my mother. I hoped trading would offer some type of distraction, but it quickly turned into another source of worry once my profits started to dip further.

My performance was poor, no doubt because my mind was elsewhere. But I also realized that I wasn't getting the same satisfaction from trading. That initial injection of euphoria I felt a few years earlier when I finally "made it" had dimmed. I'll generously compare it to when my sports idols win that first championship after years of hard work. Even if they win many more over their careers, that first will always be the pinnacle.

I was making thousands of dollars in a day, I was just collecting more cash… and, at least on paper, I already had everything I ever wanted. However, I also had to make a choice about how to deal with this law of diminishing returns.

The first option available to me was to forget about the money and focus on being the best version of myself. I was slowly slipping down the pecking order of top traders, and I wasn't happy. I could, therefore, draw my fire from that spirit of healthy competition in the office that I had loved before, and trade to the best of my ability.

The second option was a change of scenery, and a bigger payout split to blow away my trading melancholy.

I choose the latter.

The rookie-sniping renegades who had left and started an office across town offered traders a whopping 90% split of profits, compared to the 50% at my current firm. This new firm had a slightly different proprietary model, in which the trader had to provide a deposit for potential losses, which was $10k at the time. However, it still was an offer that was too good to refuse.

I felt a little guilty about abandoning my team of traders, but that had also somewhat run its course. It was no surprise that volatile Jeremy had blown up his account by then, but John and Ryan were on the cusp of becoming great traders and didn't need my help anymore.

The move seemed like it made sound financial sense, but not only would I be leaving my coaching gig, but I would also be leaving a smoothly run office that was now loaded with great traders. There were some good traders at this new office, but there wasn't much structure or a coaching program—which had both been important parts of my success, as I am too undisciplined to be left to my whims. Environment is one of the most important factors in any trader's success.

In retrospect, I am almost certain that I would have made a lot more money over my career if I had stayed at Kershner; yes, the slice of the pie would have been smaller, but I am sure the pie would have been a lot bigger. It's something to consider for any trader looking for a "better deal".

So, the move did little to restore my love of trading, and my performance continued to drop. I definitely wasn't the top dog in the office, but my whopping 90% split of my profits meant I could continue my new favorite hobby: buying stuff. I threw money at furniture for my new house, cars, holidays, eating at fancy restaurants each night, and a thousand other things. I later learned a very painful lesson about how badly miscalculated the extent of my wealth. At the time, I was sure the cash would never dry up because I was able to make thousands even though I was trading like shit.

My friends and family lived in a different world from me. They couldn't afford to join me in living the "good life", and when I tried to spread the wealth somewhat, it often made things even more uncomfortable.

Of course, I don't expect any sympathy if I whine about getting too rich too quickly, but it was a blessing and a curse. I had everything I needed–and was buying a lot of stuff that I didn't–and I still felt unsatisfied and lonely.

My relationship and new hobbies were giving me little pleasure, and trading was becoming a struggle. I was glued to a computer monitor all day while going through the continuous cycle of muted joy, and extreme agony. It all took a toll on my mind and body; I was stressed, anxious, and irritable. I needed something to numb all those feelings.

Drinking to near-addiction levels, smoking, drugs, and junk food, all seemed like good ways to take the "edge" off. For a couple of years in my mid-20s my typical daily routine consisted of: eating a big unhealthy breakfast, followed by a huge injection of caffeine provided by a couple of redneck coffees (Mountain Dew), four or five cigarette breaks to calm myself down during the trading session, further high dose injections of caffeine, and then after the close of trading, more cigarettes, beer, junk food and weed. I even started trading high occasionally. I won't share how it affected my performance, instead I will save the extensive research I have conducted on how drugs affect trading for my next book (spoiler alert.. It usually doesn't help).

Anyway, all of this wasn't healthy; I felt like a zombie and my weight ballooned. This led to me developing gout, an excruciatingly painful disease brought on by a sedentary and unhealthy lifestyle, which is rarely found in anyone under 35. I was having an early "midlife crisis" mentally, and even my body was deteriorating ahead of its years.

Amazingly, I still managed to get married (although I was high during the ceremony), finished my dream home, and brought in enough cash to support a lavish lifestyle. However, the material wealth and trips to places like Bora Bora or Hawaii did nothing, and I just felt trapped and disenchanted.

I couldn't easily change the way I felt, but I came to the realization that I could change my situation. My first action was a painful one, but I hoped it would be the seed for other positive changes to come.

After working up the courage for a few weeks, I sat Margaret down and told her that our marriage was over. I thought that we both felt something wasn't quite right but—coming out of the clear blue sky, and less than a year after our wedding—it took her by surprise. We'd never even mentioned the word divorce before. Although caught off guard, she probably assumed it was just bluster, and we would just fall back into our unhappy ways. However, I knew I had to be firm with my decision. I moved out that day, and we were officially divorced within a year.

Of course, other issues led to this first life crisis of mine (there will be more crises to come), but let me focus on the most relevant issue for this book—and that's trading and the adverse effects it can have on one's mental and physical health.

Anyone interested in trading surely has heard that success is over 90% psychological. I am somewhat of an expert in this field since I have been engaged in psychological warfare with the markets for years and have the scars to prove it.

I'm going to share a bit of my own take on the mental battles of being a trader, but I'm no psychologist. I suggest you delve further into this complex subject of trading psychology by also getting more qualified points of view. I will leave links to some of my favorite books on the subject in the resources section.

While these books—as well as certain sources on Twitter and YouTube—do a fine job of providing lessons on how to fine-tune yourself mentally to make money, they typically don't mention the toxic side effects of trading. Apart from occasional sensational stories about a trader blowing up a huge account, the dark mental side of trading is seldom mentioned. It's more pleasant to hear about traders making millions while trading on some tropical beach.

The trading education business wants to promote these success stories because they are usually hawking a paid subscription to their service. That's why little is said about the 95% who fail, and even less is spoken about the psychological trauma this business can cause.

Twenty years of experience has done little to ease that gut-wrenching feeling of having a big losing day, or trade. It's tough for a non-trader to realize the pain and anguish involved in spending a day working an extremely stressful job and ending up thousands of dollars poorer for this privilege. It's not just these losing days that can hurt. It may sound even callous, but making tens or hundreds of thousands of dollars can be just as painful or even more painful if the trader executes poorly and leaves money on the table. From my experience in the business, it seems a trader is very rarely satisfied with their performance, win or lose.

Trading can take a mental and physical toll; sitting in front of a bank of computer monitors and battling daily in an extreme game of psychological warfare against the markets is very unhealthy. I admit I may not have always managed my trading trauma most healthily, but even the most Zen-like trader cannot escape this industry without some scars. When I'm lucky enough to meet a successful trader, it's not their profits I'm impressed by—it's the fact that they have been able to survive psychologically in this brutal industry.

I've also survived where the vast majority fail. Of the 95% who don't make it as traders, most will get out relatively unscathed, or even leave better off for their experiences. Not only does trading educate one on the markets, but the psychological challenges of this industry typically leave one mentally stronger. Look at trading as an expensive course of psychotherapy, or a method to build mental toughness.

Unfortunately, others don't get so lucky. Some leave financially broken and then carry the mental trauma that naturally comes with it. Others get addicted to the rush that trading can provide and get caught chasing bigger and bigger highs. Our bodies are cruelly programmed to provide our brains with a hit of dopamine when we gamble or get into a risky trade, but it is extremely hazardous to chase that feeling with large amounts of money on the table.

I see a mild case of this addiction in some of my non-professional trading friends. A common symptom is checking their phone for crypto or stock quotes every few minutes. It gets worse when they wake up in the middle of the night to get a peek at how their positions are performing. Even more disturbing is that some of these friends are pissed even when their positions go up, complaining, "I wish I had more!"

This addiction can get a lot worse, and generally leads to financial losses, mental anguish, and dark times. I have gotten trapped in this mindset numerous times but have fortunately always found a way to escape.

A good friend of mine wasn't so lucky. He got addicted to chasing the potent highs that accompany bigger and bigger trades, resulting in him–quite predictably–wrecking his trading account. He couldn't step away, so he scraped together the funds from his family to start trading again. At first, he had a lucky streak (I say lucky because, with such a mindset, it's really just gambling) and replenished his trading account. But then the addiction kicked back in, and he continued to chase that elusive high. Losses are inevitable in such cases, and when things start to go badly wrong, things like self-sabotage, desperation, and hopelessness rear their ugly heads. The story ended tragically when he took his own life. He had some other personal issues, but I am confident he would still be alive today if it weren't for trading.

There are plenty of similar stories out there, so dealing with the psychological pressures and addictive tendencies involved with trading is an extremely serious matter. In severe cases, separating oneself from trading entirely and walking away is the only thing to do. However, professional traders who count on it for a living don't have that option. They must find ways to tackle the daily pressures of this demanding job.

There are no fail-safe solutions, but there are better alternatives than numbing yourself with drink and drugs. I'd say that my own mistakes in that area are not indicative of most of the successful long-term traders I know. In fact, when things were going so well in my former trading office in Texas, John and I were the only ones to hit up happy hour regularly. It was hardly a Wolf of Wall Street vibe. Quite the contrary, most traders were heading to the gym or church after the trading day. This, of course, is a healthier plan. And just like every trader should have a trading plan, we should all have a strategy for dealing with the sometimes toxic mental and physical side effects of this profession.

As you can tell, I've not always set the best example or had the best routines. However, from my experience, observation, and common sense, exercise and a good diet should be part of the coping plan. Meditation is also something that I, and many other traders, have adopted into our daily trading routine.

Time with loved ones and friends is a great method to relieve stress but can easily turn toxic if the pressures of trading aren't appropriately handled. Two failed marriages have harshly taught me this lesson. The psychological pressures of trading can be massive, but it's imperative not to hand this burden over to your loved ones. Instead, quality time with family and friends should help free the mind from troubles and stress and put what is truly important in life into perspective.

The older I get, the more I value time away from trading. I'm talking about both short- and long-term breaks. When you are new to the business, it's necessary to put in the hard work and get as much screen time as possible. But once you start to taste success, it's important that money doesn't become your only reward. You only have longevity if you make use of the money to find moments of freedom and independence.

Trading is an intense performance-related activity. I will compare the trader to a professional athlete again. Just as an athlete needs rest between games and a break in the offseason, the trader needs to step away from the battle now and again. I'm always looking for trends in my P&L data, and a consistent trend I have found is a spike in my profits after a prolonged (more than a few days) break from trading. Regeneration works in the short and long term: it helps one perform better but also means one can sustain a tough career over a number of years.

To get a full bang for your buck from your investment, make sure your break isn't spent checking quotes or wrapped in regret over the trades one is missing. Separate yourself from the markets and take time to really relax.

Each trader will have a different approach to handling the rigors of this sometimes toxic business, but it is imperative to have a plan. I don't have all the answers, but here's a quick reminder of what you might consider when drawing up your strategy:

- Recognize that trading is a tough mental business and don't take it lightly. Practice meditation and, at the very least, try not to switch your mind off from trading for hours each day.
- Long hours at the desk can be detrimental to your eyes, back, and body. Physical exercise is as important as mental downtime. You don't want gout in your mid-twenties!
- Junk food and energy drinks might give you the buzz to get through a day, but they aren't good fuel for a longer career. I have found an inverse relationship between my P&L and my weight over the years–the fatter I am, the less fat my bank account. Eating well will not only make you healthier, but there is a good chance it will also make you richer.
- Drinking and drugs can take the edge off when the pressure gets too much. But they are not a good crutch and definitely don't help decision-making.
- Take breaks each day, as well as short trips and longer holidays, to completely get away from the stress of trading.
- As you get further into your career, the buzz of those early wins starts to fade. Chasing the rush is a desperately dangerous path and can lead to financial and mental ruin. Understand that as you progress, you don't just keep upping the stakes to get a rush.
- A healthy relationship with trading means realizing its place in the scheme of things. Treat it as a job, not as a means of self-validation.
- Money cannot buy happiness. Even if you are having success as a trader, family, friends, health, and other passions are what truly matter.
- If you find yourself overwhelmed by the pressures of trading and you can't make that change, the most courageous thing to do sometimes is just to walk away.

10.
Missing and Taking Opportunities: Glitches Can't Buy You Love

Cutting a losing trade is the hardest part of the game. It takes courage to admit we were wrong, and the longer it takes to admit our mistake and cut the loss, the worse things typically get. Staying in that losing trade brings not only financial losses and mental anguish but also distracts us from better opportunities.

This is actually a universal truth that applies to other businesses, gambling, interactions with others, and our personal relationships. When we realize that things are not working out, the best action usually is to cut our loser and move on.

My marriage to Margaret was not working out. I'm not labeling her as a loser. On the contrary, I was a "loser", and the relationship was destined to fail because of me. I needed to be courageous and cut it before things got worse.

Margaret wasn't a soulless financial instrument; she had feelings, and she was shocked, upset, and angry when I left. I imagine she was also embarrassed in front of friends and acquaintances, and her family, who had just paid a lot of money for a lavish wedding. I knew I was doing the right thing, but it was hard to see her suffer like that.

The breakup was traumatic for me as well. My world changed overnight, and I was dealing with guilty feelings about what I had done to Margaret, wounded pride at having a marriage that didn't last a year, and fear of the unknown future. However, these were mixed with pride that I had done the hard thing and taken control of the situation, as well as a new energy bursting from within. I felt invigorated and confident—finally having rediscovered my lust for life. It was just sad that it took a divorce—and all the damage that it causes—for me to reach this point of personal epiphany.

I quickly shed 25 pounds of weight and found myself less dependent on alcohol, drugs, and unhealthy food. After a swift and painless divorce settlement, I was able to keep the house that had been destined to be a bachelor pad. I spent more time there with friends and found myself spending less money. I wasn't living like a monk, but the grips of consumerism had loosened. Instead of buying all that "stuff", I was investing the cash that came from my savings into having a good time and traveling. It didn't feel like a waste. As they say, traveling soothes the soul and broadens the mind.

However, divorce doesn't come cheap, so I needed to get back to the office and start trading after a few months of trips. By 2006, the Volatility Index (VIX) was hitting all-time lows, making it one of the slowest markets in history. As volatility disappeared, traders were also vanishing—scared off by the dead market and the evil trading bots. As a result, I returned to a much quieter office with more than a few empty desks.

Trading was tough, as the bots were sucking the life out of all available glitches. I turned to my dependable lagging plays, which even worked in the quietest of markets. I would also focus on individual stocks that I could tape read, look for repeating patterns, and then scalp back and forth. I was able to survive feeding off these simple niche strategies and the occasional glitch play. However, it was tough attritional trading, with the goal of only survival. Dreams of six- and seven-figure months seemed far, far away!

No doubt, the money still appealed to me, but it was the excitement that I really missed in this comatose market. With no end in sight to the market doldrums, I started to think about escaping this now morgue-like office and moving up the trading food chain to become one of those power brokers I'd seen prowling the streets of London. I still dreamed of strutting in my tailored suit to an exciting job at a prestigious hedge fund laden with a fat salary and an even fatter yearly bonus.

I had my freedom, as well as a British passport and some experience in the financial markets. All I really needed was the courage to say, "fuck it!" and chase this dream of mine. When the scorching Austin summer came, the heat was enough to light a fire under my ass. I rented my house, packed a couple of suitcases, and set off to England in search of adventure, following a similar path that my mom took 30 years prior.

The summer of 2007 marked the beginning of my first and most successful London sojourn. Upon arriving, I quickly found an apartment in an old converted factory in the suburb of Greenwich. Surrounded by history, high finance, and colorful characters from all corners of the globe, I felt like I was in heaven. I took time to enjoy my new life, exploring the capital and taking advantage of being a couple of hours away from so many other amazing European cities. I also spent time with my English family, polished up my accent, and joined a rugby team (finding out the hard way why American football players wear pads).

I have fond memories from those days; life was good, and I remember thinking that the icing on the cake would be landing a plum job at a hedge fund or prestigious bank. With this in mind, I put a resume together, fluffing up my job skills and qualifications: "Hitting misplaced stock orders" became "Systematic arbitrage execution", "Buying $MMM if the market goes up" became "Correlative quantitative systems expert" and "Having a daily loss limit" became "Risk management system implementation".

No dice. London is the home to many of the brightest and most skilled financial professionals in the world. These hedge fund jobs I was chasing were looking for Oxford or Cambridge graduates with experience at places like Goldman Sachs or JP Morgan, not some middling day trader with a degree from Texas Tech. With my email inbox empty and my phone silent, I realized that the doors to this vaunted dream world of mine were being slammed in my face.

Left with no real options, I keep on trading. Maybe it was a blessing in disguise because, instead of slaving away working 80 hours a week as a hedge fund trainee/slave, I got to enjoy London, travel, and have a good time. Unfortunately, traveling and living in London is not cheap, especially at this time, when the exchange rate was at $2 to £1!

One big perk of my move to London was trading from a hospitable time zone. Working from Texas meant tackling the busiest part of the trading day, the opening of the markets, sometimes half-asleep; I can't even imagine how hellish things must be trading from the west coast time zone. Trading from Europe means having my mornings free and feeling mentally sharper when the markets open in the afternoon. Picking a time zone to maximize performance and suit one's lifestyle is an excellent hack for any remote independent traders out there—just be careful about picking one of the most expensive places in the world to trade from.

I needed every edge to keep me mentally sharp when trading in mid-2008. The markets were still dead, and sloppiness was cruelly punished. Thankfully, I managed to grind out enough profits that spring and summer to cover my living expenses.

Finally, at the tail end of the summer of 2008, the markets began to wake from their slumber. There were whispers of problems in the housing market, and by autumn, these whispers had become screams. The markets went into full panic mode, causing an explosion in volatility. Of course, I wasn't prepared for this, and it seemed nobody else was either. For almost five years, the VIX– otherwise known as "the gauge of fear"–had been resting under 20. Within a month, it shot from 20 to 50! Things were getting very interesting, this was exactly what I had been waiting for, so now it was time to strap in and make some serious cash!

Unfortunately, trading out of a 200-year-old flat with a slow internet connection meant I was ill-equipped to battle this insane market. In hindsight, I should have jumped on the first plane back to Texas and joined John and the rest of the crew in my comfy old office. The ability to trade in a professional office stocked with top-notch traders is oftentimes priceless. This was one of those times, but I think I was a little shell-shocked when this all happened. I had never even seen the VIX over 40, but by October 2008, it hit 80. Things were absolutely crazy; huge global banks were going bankrupt, and there was talk of a total global financial collapse.

One of these banks that failed was Lehman Brothers. I lived just across the river from their headquarters and decided to take a walk there the day it officially collapsed to inspect the carnage. Away from the camera crews and the teary workers filing out of the office with boxes of personal belongings, things felt quite eerie. There was no blood in the streets, but I sensed plenty of fear in my beloved London. Politicians and the central banks did little to alleviate this fear, struggling to come to grips with the enormity of this economic catastrophe that was wiping out housing values, jobs, and retirement savings.

On the other hand, traders like myself were in a state of euphoria.

I would never have imagined a year earlier that many of the world's largest financial institutions would be fighting for their lives and liquidating assets. This involved them dropping huge sell orders on an already illiquid and fearful market. To compound things, many of the automated trading programs tied to these institutions had their plugs pulled. The bots were getting hammered just like everyone else, and the only way to stop the bleeding was to turn them off. This further eroded liquidity, only adding to the turbulence in these already crazy markets.

As I explained earlier in the book, the "easy" way to make money in this market—and most other turbulent markets I have witnessed—is by taking advantage of glitches. Yes, these colossal market moves provided plenty of opportunities for a skilled momentum trader, but that's assuming that trader is on the right side of the market move because one misstep in a volatile market can be deadly. Glitches take away that need for speculating. There is no more "I think it will go up" or "I think it's weak". Traders just need to find and then mechanically execute a strategy that has plenty of edge.

The turbulence tested not only the structure of the global financial system but also the structure of the markets. The U.S equity market generally held up pretty well, but there were still leaks in the pipes holding this market together, which provided many lucrative opportunities for glitch hunters—including the one shared by that generous trader back in Texas who allowed other traders to suddenly enjoy those must-dreamed-of six- and seven-figure days!

The scene was quite different in my flat in London. I was not becoming an instant millionaire. John was feeding me tales of the gargantuan trades in the Texas office, but I was working alone with a sluggish internet connection. My lagging strategies came alive, and I did make some money off auction strategies, but I was settling for six-figure months instead of six-figure days.

These were my most profitable months ever, but they also represent some of the worst trading mistakes of my career. A trader should always step up their game during the good times, but I was not aggressive enough and missed huge opportunities. I also broke another cardinal trading rule by trading stubbornly. I was extremely fortunate to be handed the key to easy riches when John passed this secret auction strategy on to me, but instead of milking it, I stuck to my own less lucrative strategies. Perhaps it would have helped if I was in the Austin office with those guys, but regardless, I knew the strategy, I knew the basic execution, and I knew there was plenty of edge. My stubbornness was inexcusable and regrettable, especially considering my future financial troubles.

If my cowardly and stubborn trading, and my decision to trade remotely from London, wasn't costly enough, at the height of all this madness, I met a beautiful young woman from Poland. She was in her early twenties, gorgeous and fun.

I immediately fell madly in love. Ania had put me in a daze, becoming the only thing that mattered to me; the ridiculous trading opportunities were just an afterthought. Just after we met, I recklessly took her on a date during market hours. On returning, I asked John if I had missed any good opportunities while I was gone, and he replied that he had made 400K. Expensive date!

Right before I met Ania, I had finally come to my senses and made the prudent financial decision to move back to Texas, at least temporarily. So, in November 2008, I left London as planned and headed to Austin–but now with vacationing Ania in tow. My plans of returning to Austin and making some serious cash had changed to showing Ania a good time in my hometown. I only made it to the office once, and not even to trade! It was just a stop off on our sightseeing tour. When I dropped in, I wasn't the only spectator, it seemed other traders' friends and family had also squeezed into this cramped and sweaty office to witness this spectacle.

I was in awe of the buzzing atmosphere and the obscene amount of cash being made—these guys were rockstars! It was indeed quite a sight to see, a room full of guys in their 20s with chests puffed out, making small, or in many cases large, fortunes in mere seconds. It was impressive, but I must have been out of my mind because it still wasn't tempting enough for me to leave my girl for half an hour a day and join in on all the fun.

Before you throw down this book in utter disgust, let me tell you that there is at least a happy ending. I didn't come to my senses and start making millions, but I did get the girl. During our stay, Ania agreed to move to Austin with me.

"Lucky in cards, unlucky in love" is how the saying goes. In my case, it's been "lucky in trading, unlucky in love," and vice versa. This is backed up by the astonishing statistic that 95% of my trading profits have come in the 50% of my trading career when I haven't been married. However, that is really a stat that I throw out there a little facetiously... the truth is that the Global Financial Crisis of 2008 and the COVID panic of 2020/21 coincided with periods in which I was unmarried. It seems global suffering, rather than individual suffering has the greatest correlation with trading profits.

So this isn't a cautionary tale against the danger of mixing women and trading, quite the contrary—a healthy relationship should only benefit one's trading. I actually want to focus on the importance of taking advantage of trading opportunities when the going is good. Even with the "Great Ania Distraction of 2008", I still made exponentially more money in these two periods, when the markets were going nuts, than the rest of my career combined. Any successful trader you ask would probably have a similar story.

I thought I traded well throughout 2019. I worked hard, stayed fairly disciplined, stuck to my strategies, and subsequently didn't have a losing month. Then came March 2020, and I made more in a few days than I had made during the whole of the previous year while busting my ass. Honestly, if you want to be a millionaire trader someday, you won't make all that money by grinding out 10k months for years on end. You make it by being ready, smart, and courageous when the really big opportunities come along–just like those rookie traders in Texas who made millions in a few weeks in 2008, while I was wining and dining in London.

It's not just broad market panics like those in 2008 and 2020 that offer opportunities for huge windfalls for traders. I have seen traders come into the office in Texas for half an hour, three or four times a year, and make more than a well-paid executive. These crafty traders only appeared when a specific "trading event" was happening; examples of such "trading events" for equity day traders include an index rebalancing, a highly anticipated IPO, a flash crash, a big news play, volatility in a specific sector, or some other type of glitch play. A specific example of one of these "trading events" was the Tesla closing auction trade I mentioned earlier, during which some traders made millions in seconds.

The amount of time one spends trading typically has little correlation with profits. Actually, during the slow times, the more time I spend in front of my screens, the worse my results are. The problem is that these slow times seem like they last for an eternity, making the wait for this volatility excruciating. The 12 years between the madness of 2008 and that of 2020 were some of the least volatile times in the markets history, sucking the life out of many promising trading careers–thus depriving them of the opportunity to cash in when the big opportunities finally came. It was tragic to see many decent traders get wiped out just before they had the chance to ride giant waves of volatility to almost certain riches.

Surviving these prolonged market lulls means having a strategy, or two, to grind out some consistent profits, making enough cash to keep the trading account flush, and keeping one's confidence buoyant. Even during these lulls, there are plenty of opportunities for a skilled trader, and these intermittent "trading events" can even provide opportunities for big paydays. For experienced traders with fat trading accounts (i.e., those "trading event" part-time traders in Texas), there is also the option of playing golf and sailing yachts during the slow times, and then jumping back ashore when things get interesting.

When such a "trading event" comes along, you need to be ready, be in the right environment, and you need to have a plan to take advantage of the opportunities. These events usually require due diligence and the confidence to "go big" and trade aggressively to maximize profit fast. Things get a little more complicated If we are talking about trading in a highly volatile market, like those of 2008 and 2020. In this case, the trader should adjust their trading plan, adopting a different and more aggressive line of attack than when battling a tranquil market, and, most importantly, don't fall in love so hard that it turns your head from market conditions that come along only a couple of times in a whole trading career!

11.
Bear Markets:
Poland Calling

Bears and trading have peculiarly been linked together through the years. A "bear market" is a familiar term to nearly all traders, describing a steady and prolonged market decline. You might think that the powerful bear would be associated with strength and domination; however, according to Investopedia, the term comes from the way that a bear swipes its claw downwards—and you know that when it does, it can rip your insides out!

While these majestic animals provide a colorful way to describe the markets, I think they can serve the trader even more if we copy their behavior. In preparation for the winter, the bear is biologically programmed to feast and get as fat as possible during the lush and plentiful spring and summer months. The bear doesn't know how long or how harsh this winter might be, so every extra ounce of fat might mean the difference between death or survival.

The trader should adopt a similar mindset; gorging on profits when the markets are bountiful in order to survive the inevitable lean times. Back in 2008, If I had known the approaching lean times would last for over ten years, I would have concentrated more on feasting.

As the year wound down, my pockets weren't as fat as they should have been, but I had at least found a mate. My whirlwind romance with Ania took us from meeting in London to living in my (now our) den by the lake in Texas, with a quick stop-off in Paris for a marriage proposal.

When I had left the Austin office a year or so earlier, I considered myself one of the better traders on the trading floor. I returned way down the pecking order; the office had been gorging on profits while I dithered, dated, and underachieved in London. Word of the success in the office—and of all those newly minted millionaires—had spread. Trading was in vogue again and the office was packed with cash-hungry opportunists. Sadly, this is a lagging phenomenon because when all the fresh blood hits the trading floor, it typically means the good times are over. In fact, my return to the office coincided with the beginning of a long, long winter—the panic abated, and the market volatility plummeted.

It was tough for us to complain about the market rebound since we had just been treated to some of the highest market volatility levels ever recorded. Even people like myself, who had not made the most of every moment, had been afforded trading opportunities beyond our wildest dreams. We were almost to the point that if the markets had continued to crash, we would have been living in a dystopian world run by day traders. Thankfully for humanity, the markets bounced with capitalism still intact.

Initially, I used this market lull as an excellent excuse to get back on the road and show my new fiancée the rest of America—making sure my profits from 2008 weren't wasting away in a boring bank account.

Keeping with the frantic pace of the relationship (and my life in general), Ania was pregnant within a couple of months of us moving to Texas. We were both ecstatic, and knowing we would have to settle down soon, we planned one last big trip to Europe for a traditional Polish wedding and some more traveling. No one does a wedding quite like the Polish. It's a marathon, not a sprint. My English and American family members lacked endurance and struggled to match the vodka-drinking prowess of Ania's Polish family. Still, all in attendance had a great time, despite the massive hangovers. Capping off the trip, we (Ania, me, and the big bump in her belly) headed to Italy and Croatia for a honeymoon.

Our 2009 had also been a marathon, traveling and making the very most of life. Settling back down in Texas meant enjoying time with my new wife and our amazing baby daughter, Zuza. I also re-dedicated myself to trading, which I was excited to do despite the continuing decompression of market volatility. I felt I had underperformed in 2008 and wanted to prove myself again. I knew that a familiar office, surrounded by some of the best traders in the game, was the right place for me to do it... even if everything seemed to be against possible success.

These sudden tranquil markets provided fertile hunting grounds for the resilient trading bots, who had reasserted their dominance and had become fine-tuned cash-printing monsters, leaving little scraps for us old-school scavengers to feed on. These are the times when a trader should re-evaluate the landscape, tread cautiously, look for new strategies, and adjust their trading plan to the tune of the changing market conditions.

It was a treacherous time for those newer traders who hit the jackpot in 2008. With their confidence sky-high, and only faint memories of how challenging trading can be, very few of these fortunate souls were willing to step off the throttle and gently apply the brakes. Those who kept gunning it ended up hitting a brick wall and giving back a sizable chunk (or sometimes all) of their profits.

This type of recklessness is typical after any wave of great trading: naivety, stubbornness, overconfidence, and a lack of discipline are the main culprits behind this behavior. It was tough to call me naive, but I was guilty of those other three and ended up losing a decent amount of my profits from the year before. In fact, 2009 was my first losing year since my rookie campaign.

Ania had trouble settling in Texas, missing her family and Europe in general. I didn't blame her. She had a baby daughter and had been slotted into my life in Texas; my house, my friends, my family. It must have been tough. I also missed the buzz of London and the European lifestyle. So, with this in mind, and considering that trading from the office hadn't brought me the luck I had expected, we decided to set out on another adventure and move back to London.

John bought our house, which was a blessing. I was happy to keep it in the family, and we sorely needed the cash. My poor long-term investing skills, and poor money management, meant we had already burned through most of my savings, and with no income coming in, I needed to give myself some buffer while I tried to reinvigorate my sluggish trading. In hindsight, leaving an office stocked with great traders and heading to one of the most expensive cities in the world to do things remotely wasn't the best way to protect those already dwindling reserves.

We arrived back in London in the summer of 2010 with a few suitcases and a 6-month-old baby in tow. We moved to a lovely apartment in Greenwich—in a converted Victorian school—just around the corner from my previous pad.

It was good to be back in London, but I wasn't there to see the sights. I needed to get to work.

I found a couple of fellow traders from Canada who wanted to share an office. We set up shop together in my beloved City of London, trading out of a dingy office only a stone's throw away from the mammoth trading floors that shaped the global markets. Louis, Francois, and I were well aware of our position at the bottom of the trading food chain. Despite our standing, we still felt some type of fraternity with the traders working in the fancy offices of prestigious firms: those whales were still feeding in the same waters as us bottom feeders.

In Texas, my commute consisted of driving through the suburbs, then passing by a few strip malls before reaching a characterless commercial office park. Now in London, I strolled through an area once populated by legions of Roman traders. The Romans made way for the armies of modern-day traders that now patrol these ancient roads positioned in the center of the financial world. On my pleasurable commute, I would soak in the energy reverberating through the great city, longing to be a legendary trader like those gods sitting up on those gilded trading floors standing above me in the sky.

The problem was I lacked the legendary strategies that create legendary traders. Volatility was now just an afterthought, and the trading bots had suffocated the familiar glitches. Copying winning strategies from the Austin office or Louis and Francois wasn't a viable option either, since it seemed every trader had similar struggles. I needed to unearth some golden strategies and find myself a new niche.

Every trader should have a niche, and I will define having a niche as having a specific trading style and strategies. The problem is that most traders don't understand the definition of "specific". Typically, when I ask a trader what their primary strategy is, I hear something like, "I trade stocks that are breaking out" or "I trade Biotechs". I want to hear something like, "I trade biotech stocks with a high short float that are breaking yearly highs during the first ten minutes of trading" – now that's a niche!

With so many trading styles and instruments to choose from, a trader without focus will easily get lost (i.e., blown up). Focus means tackling the treacherous game of trading by finding a specific style and a few accompanying strategies, and then sharpening your skills by executing the same strategies repeatedly and mechanically. Juggling too much only results in sloppy execution and missed opportunities. Don't be the equivalent of that restaurant owner who serves Chinese, American, and Mexican food; instead, focus on one cuisine and on cooking up just a few exceptional recipes.

Of course, what style and strategies you choose as your niche are essential. The most important thing is that this niche has an edge; if you execute these niche strategies efficiently, will you make money? Don't open that Chinese restaurant because you like that food; open it because it will make you money.

That's not to say you shouldn't consider your personal traits and predisposition as a trader when developing your niche. If you are slow on the keyboard, look for strategies that don't rely on speed; if you are a bottom picker, don't look for strategies that revolve around breakouts. Keep in mind that just like restaurants can hire chefs to cook their recipes, traders can also get chefs (bots) to cook (execute) their recipes (strategies). But if you are going to do things the traditional way, and cook up your own recipes, don't open a Chinese restaurant if you are awful at cooking Chinese food!

That makes me a boring and straightforward guy since my strategies, such as my lagging plays, have typically been simple and uncomplicated; my niches are more English food than Chinese. The Great British cookbook consists of straightforward dishes like fish and chips, and I have survived 20-plus years in the trading game on the equivalent of such plain and simple fayre.

This boring approach of mine has meant months, or even years, spent focusing on a specific sector or stock. For a couple of years during the mid-2000s, I focused on scalping one obscure stock that almost nobody had heard of–the ultra-high-dollar homebuilder stock, $NVR. It perfectly fit my style because I loved expensive stocks, and $NVR tended to move slowly, just like me. What made $NVR even more appealing was that it lagged its sector and was relatively free of bots, allowing me to utilize my tape reading skills and continually hone my strategy over time.

Although I was enamored, I wasn't blindly loyal to my darling $NVR. I always had a wandering eye, looking for glitches or searching for something more lucrative. The ups and downs of my P&L made it a rocky relationship, but I stayed loyal and committed enough to make it quite fruitful over the years.

Another niche of mine throughout the years has been trading volatility ETNs (Exchange traded notes) such as $VXX and $UVXY. My original plan was simply to short these glitchy stocks, knowing they have a flaw in their structure, which means they perpetually go down. How do I know this? Well, their prospectus graciously points this out, definitively stating: "If you hold your ETNs as a long-term investment, it is likely you will lose all or a substantial portion of your investment". The prospectus has turned out to be prophetic, with $UVXY losing 99.99% of its value over the years, going from $2 billion to $10 in the last ten years! That's no typo, and tragically I didn't cash in on this monstrous move, instead of simply shorting $VXX or $UVXY, I developed more complicated, and ultimately less lucrative strategies. Despite my missteps, I have had success trading these volatility ETNs, and recommend that traders familiarize themselves with these ETNs and the volatility complex in general.

Disclaimer - I'm not recommending blindly shorting $UVXY. Do your homework first.

It doesn't have to be a particular stock or sector; it could be a specific—and I mean REALLY specific—technical setup or a "trading event" one chooses to focus on. For example, one of the most profitable strategies of many traders I know has been to buy the opening trade of an IPO (initial public offering). Sounds easy, right? Well, just like any other strategy, it only works if the trader has a detailed plan and skillful execution (In the next chapter, we will discover that sometimes that's not even enough).

Trading a specific glitch would be considered a niche, and in my book (this book), glitches are the best place to turn when looking for a niche. It is also one area where I will make an exception to the rule of finding a niche that fits your personality because sometimes these glitches have so much edge and so much reward that it's worth trying to adapt your style to trade these golden strategies. Again, your P&L totals are the ultimate judge of whether a strategy is worth implementing into your training plan.

Back in London, I was trying to find a new and profitable niche. They do exist even in the most challenging markets but may be a little harder to find and require more patience and skill to execute. In slow markets, the potential winnings are also less spectacular, and things take time. Finding a niche can also be a costly process. Losses are inevitable as you develop ideas and invest in some hunches and potential paths to success that don't work out.

Although there were spells of volatility—especially during the Euro debt crisis of 2011—times were tough. To compound my problems, I wasn't trading with discipline or particularly skillfully; A great strategy is worthless without efficient execution. I was also overcomplicating things—essentially trying to cook complicated and exotic recipes instead of good old fish and chips.

With my losses piling up, and my savings dwindling down, I would typically leave the office utterly dejected, stumbling past pubs packed with what I assumed were joyous financial professionals celebrating their daily haul. I longed to be part of that tribe—mostly because I was losing my own money and about to go broke.

It was time to bombard the city again with my inflated resume. The embellishments were still present, but this resume now included my 2008 P&L total, which I thought would wow potential employers. Although that number was minuscule compared to what some traders had made during the same period, I still thought it looked impressive on paper. I just hoped suspicions wouldn't be raised since I had left off my 2009 total.

As I explained earlier, be wary of any supposedly successful trader who is willing to share golden secrets for a small fee. Another thing to be on the lookout for is a supposedly successful trader looking to join the civilian workforce. It's extremely rare for any trader who makes a consistent profit to walk away for a lower-paid salaried job in which they are expected to work regular hours, answer to a boss, and have zero chance of making a million dollars in a month. The financial firms in London are obviously a lot smarter than all of the suckers who shell out their cash for "golden secrets", so the bait sat there untouched. They could spot a struggling trader from a mile away– meaning that my potential escape route from the struggle of trading was cut off.

Nothing came easy during this period. Ania was pregnant again and even our precious Milla did things the difficult way by arriving into the world in the back of the car on the way to the hospital. Ania delivered the baby by herself in the back of a moving vehicle while I clung onto the wheel and drove as best I could. It's very much a metaphor for how my career was at the time!

John and the rest of the trading crew in Texas also found the going tough. In fact, the whole day-trading industry was suffering. One of the bigger proprietary trading firms, Schonfeld Securities, fired a big chunk of their trading floor and fired off a letter with an ominous warning that sent chills through the industry,

"Unfortunately, our vision of the future of trading has changed. It is getting much tougher for traders to make a living or get by. The direct competition from black boxes, stat arb and high frequency trading which continues to grow at exponential rates is here to stay and has caused us to change our outlook for lesser skilled traders. Based on the above competitive changes to the trading arena, we feel we are doing an injustice to both our lesser skilled traders and the firm by keeping them around. At best, they will barely get by and that's not why we are in this business or what they should be here for. Unfortunately the career of trading is not a good option for lesser skilled traders going forward."

2011 had been another poor year for me, so I was firmly entrenched in this category of "lesser skilled traders" that the note referred to. I had somehow blown through seven figures of profits from the last decade, so with our savings almost depleted, and no income to talk of, things were getting dire. With no other options, I had to fight, and it became imperative to make some cash. The stress involved in trading is pretty immense, even with a bloated bank account; however, the stress of trading with no confidence and one's back against the wall is almost immeasurable.

Feeling ashamed and guilty that I had gotten us into this precarious situation and not wanting her to go through the same angst I was suffering, Ania was in the dark about the real state of our finances. I genuinely thought I would somehow dig us out of our deepening hole, but I hit full panic mode as the summer of 2012 approached. With only a few months of savings left, I knew something drastic had to be done immediately.

Let me flashback to when I was a young boy, growing up just 20 miles downriver in Essex, and to the day when my mom broke the news to us kids that we were moving west to America, "The Land of Opportunity", and her original home. I remember initially being shocked and upset by the news, maybe even a little frightened. However, my mood lightened once mom reassured us that everything was going to be okay and that we would even go on a road trip exploring America. The icing on the cake was when she told us the plan was to get a nice house with our own swimming pool.

In 2012, I went to my wife with a somewhat similar proposal. Even though I would have struggled to place Poland on a map a few years prior, and even though the flow of migration is typically in the other direction, I suggested to Ania that we move to her homeland (which, crucially has a cost of living which is much lower than in the UK), and that we did so immediately. I also tried to reassure her that everything would be ok, but I definitely couldn't promise a swimming pool, or for that fact, even our own house. All I could promise was a long road trip. Ania was surprisingly receptive, so we packed our belongings and headed off on our road trip. This time I wasn't exploring the coast of California, but instead heading with my young family to rural Poland, to move in with my mother-in-law.

12.

A Final Blow: I.P.Ow!

A couple of years earlier, it would have been tough to imagine going from living the high life in my dream home on the lake in Texas to moving in with my mother-in-law in her small Communist-styled apartment in the fields of rural Poland. It was quite an impressive turn of fortune, and it was all my own damn fault: I had traded like a fool, passed on amazing strategies and opportunities, managed my savings terribly, and operated with no backup plan for when things went sour.

Let me concentrate on the last of those mistakes, because attempting to be a professional trader without a backup plan is pure folly—a point that I want to nail into every trader and prospective trader's head. It's like skydiving without a reserve parachute, and while the potential consequences for the unprepared skydiver are typically grimmer, the odds of catastrophe for a trader are astronomically higher. Regardless of if you are an experienced or novice trader, at some point you will make a mistake or get caught out by the market and, if you don't have that reserve 'chute, it's inevitable that you will hit the ground face first.

Having a big pile of cash to fall into will always soften the blow, of course. There are some traders who have already made enough money that they can absorb a hit. For the others who don't have that luxury, a "reserve parachute" means having an alternative means of income. And that doesn't just mean having other trades that might come good. A good trader will have a backup that is either a nice stream of passive income, such as property rental, or a legitimate alternative profession or monetizable skills that he or she can move into if things go horribly wrong.

Because I didn't have any of those things, I entered a fiscal freefall and endured a rough landing in Poland. I then had to pick myself up, dust myself off, get to work, and make some cash. Having no other skills or passive income that I could fall back upon, I felt like my only option was to try to trade my way out of the situation. What's more, I was trying to do it from my mother-in-law's apartment equipped with intermittent internet, and with crying kids at my side. After a valiant attempt, I packed it in and instead went for walks in the countryside and introduced my kids to farmyard animals.

Pretty soon after we got to Poland, I received news that finally offered some hope, suggesting the trading gods might be ready to show me some mercy. Back then, one of the only remaining strategies that seemed to provide any edge revolved around initial public offerings (IPOs). The basic idea of the strategy was to buy the opening trade on the day a company became public (or had their IPO) and then sell immediately in the ensuing euphoria, or "pump". Typically, the more hype around the IPO, the better the results. There wasn't any company in the world at this time that was more hyped than Facebook and–after years of rumors and anticipation–in the spring of 2012, Facebook finally announced its IPO. The buzz was deafening.

Even though the actual trade would only last seconds or minutes, I knew that I had to fly halfway around the world and to the safe confines of the Austin office. Although we were almost broke, I was certain that this one trade was the answer to all our problems, so I considered it a shrewd investment. I needed fast and reliable internet, a proper trading setup, and, most importantly, to surround myself with elite traders who would help me get the most from the opportunity.

Arriving in Austin, it felt reassuring that the whole office shared high expectations for this IPO. We all agreed that this was the time for aggression, and despite my fragile confidence, it felt like the only option was to go all in, risking all of the meager balance left in my trading account; it was kill or be killed. I was excited, but there was nervousness, anxiety, and dread at what it would mean for my small family if it went wrong. I didn't have a backup plan.

The day of the IPO started with an ominous sign. We discovered that one of our friends had received an allocation of shares of Facebook at the offering (wholesale) price. A surprising turn of events, since only those well-connected, such as privileged hedge funds, typically receive shares of an IPO at the offering price. The fact that a friend with a small brokerage account received shares meant there wasn't the demand for these shares we expected. I knew all too well that when the small guys get handed anything from the big boys in this business, it typically means they are about to get screwed. I and the rest of the office chose to ignore this warning sign and proceeded with our plans, waiting nervously for the opening trade of Facebook on the Nasdaq exchange.

I had placed orders using every last dollar of my available capital, planning to buy the opening trade and then quickly sell on the inevitable initial surge. After an excruciating wait, it finally began trading, and our stomachs collectively sank. Upon opening, it did have a quick pump to the upside, but, within seconds, it was trading under the price of the opening trade.

This was a trade which we had all bought, or at least we thought we had all bought...But our shares hadn't appeared in our accounts! A technical problem had hit the exchange, and we had no idea if our orders had been filled or, by the grace of God, been canceled. We sat in a state of shock as the stock continued plummeting. Our office managers frantically worked the phones to no avail, leaving us in the dark for hours. With my fate hanging in the air, I paced the office and braced myself for what I assumed would be more bad news.

Finally, what we all dreaded came to pass when our Facebook shares appeared in our trading blotters. It only took a quick glance at my P&L to realize my trading account was demolished. It felt like a punch to the gut.

Facebook caused widespread destruction throughout the office. John and Mike played it even more aggressively than I, cleaning out larger accounts. John even received the honor of being interviewed by the Wall Street Journal regarding the debacle, but John's sudden stardom did little to ease our pain, we were all helpless innocent victims.

Sadly, this isn't an isolated incident, these problems happen often, and exchange-related issues are just one of the many possible "technical issues" that can cruelly wipe out an account; internet outages, software glitches, and hardware malfunctions are among the other landmines.

While I am on this unpleasant subject, I will also warn you that technical issues aren't the only things that can drain an account. I know many traders who have seen their trading accounts vanish overnight because their broker went bust. One reckless act by one reckless trader–combined with lax risk management procedures–can take down a whole firm. Unfortunately, in the unscrupulous world of shady online brokers, "bust" might also mean that the broker just ran off with their client's cash.

Every trader should be aware of this and take extreme caution in selecting a reputable broker. Precautions can be taken, but unless the broker is federally insured (unfortunately, these insured brokers generally offer inferior leverage and higher commission), the trader should get in the habit of holding their breath each time they log into their account.

So, to summarize: you can be in the lucky 5%, do everything right and make tons of cash, but still lose everything because of issues out of your control... Still want to be a trader?!

Calling Ania after the Facebook debacle, I wished I had never stepped foot in this god-forsaken profession. I broke the tragic news to her with tears streaming down my cheeks. I had let our family down and I returned to Poland defeated, with my tail behind my legs.

Ania had found a house to rent while I was gone, but we now had only a couple of months' worth of rent and bills left in our bank account. Truly desperate, I frantically searched for a job and stumbled upon an opening for a junior futures spread trader in Krakow–a city 4 hours away from our new home. Spread trading is a highly conservative and tedious form of trading and not the career path I was looking for, but beggars can't be choosers. I put my heart and soul into winning this job that would have me grouped with a bunch of 20-year-old trading neophytes, pay me a $300 monthly salary, and mean I would have to commute from Krakow to see my family.

I had been in the business for over a decade, worked on some great trading floors, and trained some fantastic traders, so I had to swallow my pride to even apply for this job. Then, a couple of days after my second trek to Krakow for my final interview, I received a rejection notice. That hurt! It was a dagger right through my heart and surely the final nail in the coffin of my trading career.

To say my mood was dark would be an understatement; I was out of options and out of cash. My only hope was to ask John for an emergency loan, but right before I went to him to beg for salvation, I received a letter that seemed to answer my prayers.

John forwarded some mail from Texas and, while scouring through it, I opened a letter from Bank of America that offered a deal that seemed too good to be true—a $35,000 cash advance loan. Bank of America didn't know I was broke and had split the country, but I was grateful for their charity nonetheless. I knew that I didn't have the means to repay the loan at that time, but to be honest, I wasn't overly concerned about the repayment—I was just desperate to support my family. One could argue the moral merits of my decision, knowing my ability and motivation to repay. However, I figured that if this giant corporation—which had just received billions in bailouts from taxpayers—was going to try to gouge me, and plenty of other poor desperate souls, with a 25% interest rate, then they deserved the risk associated with handing me this bailout, or lifeline.

Flush with my 35k in cash, a sense of sweet relief filled my stressed body. Knowing I never wanted to get myself and my family in such a desperate situation again, I had to come up with a plan to get myself one of these reserve parachutes. Unfortunately, I knew no way to bring in income other than through the path that had gotten us into our desperate situation in the first place. My recent results were dismal, but I knew there was still edge out there in the market. I figured it was only a matter of time before the next great wave of volatility hit, so with no other viable options, I replenished my trading account and set out to resurrect my career.

Still scarred from the Facebook debacle, and with open wounds from my losing battles with the markets from the previous few years, I proceeded cautiously. Tackling this tough market out of a basement in Poland, equipped with a slow internet connection, made the job even more challenging. Despite the headwinds, I traded with discipline and started to regain my confidence; feeding on glitches and my volatility niche, I put together a string of profitable months, rekindling my love affair with this profession.

If I could succeed out of my basement in Poland, then all these doomsayers must be mistaken about the future of day trading. With my spirits lifted, I concocted a plan to take full advantage of my little nest egg and the trading boom that I was sure was just around the corner.

My failed interview in Krakow came with a silver lining because it gave me another insight into the profit-making potential of these proprietary firms. They operated on a similar model to the prop firms in the U.S that I was already familiar with; providing capital for traders and, in return, taking a generous slice of these trader's profits and an even bigger cut of the commissions generated by the trader.

I know the success rate for traders is extremely low but, according to my calculations, a firm only needs one or two good traders to pay for all the other failures. This calculation took into account the average trading market, so when volatility surges and the trading is more lucrative, these firms absolutely kill it. I knew all this firsthand since I had visited the colossal mansion of the guy who owned the prop firm in Austin.

With all of this in mind, I came up with the idea of opening a small proprietary trading firm in my new hometown of Wroclaw. I was certain I knew how to make money trading, but the sad truth was that I was too undisciplined to consistently follow my rules to success. I was confident, though, that I could teach these rules and winning strategies to other traders and then share in the rewards of their success. Not only would this be my path to riches, but it would also enable me to trade from an office again and allow me to mentor people, which I had previously truly enjoyed.

The plan was to hire a small group of traders, provide them with capital, and have a payout scale that began at 50% and then worked upwards. Although I wouldn't provide any salary for these traders, it was still more than a fair deal in the prop trading world—especially since I was planning on giving them what I thought was a top-notch trading education. The whole basis of this education would revolve around discipline and keeping the losses tight, so I assumed I would only have to risk around $5,000 of capital for each trader. The rest of the overhead costs for this firm would be reasonable since Poland was so affordable; office rent, office bills, accountants, lawyers, and other such expenses were all a fraction of the cost compared to most other countries in the developed world.

Unlike U.S. firms, I could run the business through an offshore broker, enabling the traders to trade without security licenses. These offshore brokers also offered ultra-cheap commissions, providing a nice profit margin once I marked up the trader's commissions. Intraday leverage of up to 100 to 1 (for $10,000, I could have $1,000,000 to trade with) meant I didn't need a massive amount of capital. The more I crunched the numbers, the more excited I got.

After completing what I felt was a thorough business plan, I figured I would need around $75,000 to $100,000 to start this dream firm of mine. This number, of course, was ridiculously low; I'm sure most other prop firms, even the small ones, are capitalized by millions. Regardless, it was still way more than I could afford. I had about $25k sitting in my bank account that I was somewhat stupidly willing to throw down, but that still meant I needed at least another $50k from investors or partners.

After some pleading, John and Mike both agreed to match my $25K investment in return for a slice of the action. Compassion certainly played a role in their decision, considering this was a trading business run by a guy who had never run a business and had recently struggled with his own trading. The other potential investors I pitched to weren't so charitable, but I had $75k to start the business.

I was responsible for everything; recruiting, training, marketing, risk management, and accounting. I wouldn't be receiving a salary, so the onus would be on me to support my family by trading my own account; quite a challenge considering I now had only a couple of months of savings left and had been struggling even without the additional responsibility of running a business. In retrospect, it seemed quite idiotic to take on the challenge of starting an undercapitalized and undermanned prop firm while skating on thin ice with my own trading and finances, but I went full speed ahead nonetheless.

I found a professional-looking office with its own private elevator, befitting the prestigious firm I was about to build. I then blew a big part of the budget furnishing this office with ultra-fast desktop computers and big-screen monitors. Developing a training program and marketing the company were priorities, but other tasks—such as writing contracts, building a website, and designing a logo—competed for my limited time.

When the time came to find the first five traders for this prestigious firm, I was happy with the number and the quality of the applicants I received in response to my "U.S Equity Trader" job posting. Ideally, I would have filtered out the applicants by testing their skills by having them work a market stall or by trading baseball cards, but I had to settle for math and abstract reasoning tests.

Recruiting traders is far from an exact science, but these tests can give a little insight into each person's potential. Most good traders have strong math skills, and the fact that it was a timed math test gave me some indication of how the applicant reacted under pressure. Abstract reasoning tests revolve around pattern recognition, which is the basis for finding and executing strategies in trading, so I also find this test helpful.

My first round of group interviews also allowed me to sell my vision to these lucky youngsters.

After their tests, I would stand in front of the group in my freshly bought "Wall Street CEO" outfit, extolling the virtues of being a professional trader. My job was to be the hype man; "You can be the next millionaire trader! Live the good life, travel the world, and work when you please!" It was also my job to try and sell them that I was one of these baller traders, which was quite a stretch considering my recent trading results. However, I didn't feel too guilty for overselling this image because I thought I was offering a fantastic opportunity to these applicants. Regardless of my recent run of form, I still had the experience, connections, and capital to give these traders a half-decent shot at succeeding. As we know by now, a "half-decent shot" is about as good as it gets in this business and is a hell of a lot better than the 0% shot if they attempted the challenge alone.

I considered the applicants' scores on the tests and brushed over their resumes. I was mostly looking for confidence and competitiveness; I was searching for swagger. I wanted someone who had no doubts that they could succeed and flourish in this cutthroat world. When it was all said and done, I was pleased with the group of five I had assembled and sure that there was a legendary trader among them. Maybe it was the chess prodigy? Or the 18-year-old gamer? The math genius? Or perhaps the American expat who had somehow ended up in Wroclaw? Maybe all of them…

13.

Raising the Stakes:
C.R.E.A.M.

The Cream Capital Group was ready to be unleashed. "Cash rules everything around me!" is Method Man's proclamation on my favorite Wu-Tang Clan track, 'C.R.E.A.M'. This acronym and the shortened chant of "Cash Rules!" are familiar to all hip-hop fans. On this grimy street anthem, Raekwon The Chef brags about making that "cream" and how his "slick ass clique" made "40 G's" in a week. Cash and bluster also rule in the trading business—bragging about "making 40 G's in a week" is just as likely to be heard coming from the lips of a trader than from the mic of an MC—so I thought Cream Capital Group (threw the "Capital" in there for some Wall Street cred) was a perfect name for my "slick ass clique" of traders.

In both trading and the rap game, confidence is key to making that cream. I needed my clan dripping in swagger, just like my Wu-Tang heroes. It was also imperative that their leader exude confidence. My job was to make these guys believe I had the tools, knowledge, and know-how to turn them into millionaires. With this in mind, I christened our first day at the office with what I thought was a hell-raising speech, modeled straight from the legendary address Ben Affleck gives to his group of trainees in the movie 'Boiler Room', that goes like this:

"This is the deal. I am not here to waste your time and I can only hope you're not here to waste mine. So I'm gonna keep this short. You become an employee of this firm and you will make your first million within three years. Okay?

"Let me repeat that. You will make a million dollars within three years of your first day of employment at JT Marlin. Everybody got that? There is no question as to whether you will be a millionaire working at this firm, the question is how many times over.

"You think I'm joking? I am not joking. I am a millionaire. It's a weird thing to hear, right? I'll tell you, it's a weird thing to say. I'm a fucking millionaire. Now guess how old I am? Twenty-seven. You know what that makes me here? A fucking senior citizen. This firm is entirely composed of people your age, not mine. Lucky for me, I am very fucking good at my job or I'd be out of one. You guys are the new blood. You're gonna go home with the kesef. You're the future Big-Swinging-Dicks of this firm.

"Now you all look money hungry and that's good. Anybody who says money is the root of all evil, doesn't have it! Money can't buy happiness? Look at the fucking smile on my face. Ear to ear, baby. You wanna hear details? I drive a Ferrari 355 cabriolet. I have a ridiculous house on the South Fork. I've got every toy you can imagine. And best of all, kids, I am liquid.

"So now that you know what's possible, let me tell you what's required. You are required to work your ass off. We want winners, not pikers. A piker is someone who walks at the bell. A piker asks how much vacation time he gets in the first year. See, people work here to become filthy rich. No other reason. That's it. You want vacation time? Go teach third grade public school."

My version of the speech was watered down a bit, I didn't have it in me to tell them I was a multi-millionaire—and substituting Toyota Camry for Ferrari 355 wouldn't have had the same ring—but I felt like I still made a strong impression on my crew of rookies.

After taking to their new desks and logging on to demo accounts on their shiny new computers, I soon realized that one of the traders, my American compatriot, had not digested my stirring speech. Upon entering his first trade on the demo account, he started screaming "Oh maaaan!" and "Fuck me!" in response to every single penny swing. His cries echoed throughout the office like a wounded animal.

Unfortunately, the fate of a wounded animal and a wild trader is typically the same. The humane thing to do in both cases is to end their suffering as soon as possible. Lacking the discipline to control one's emotions is a kiss of death in this business. The greatest traders that I have met aren't wild; they are cold-blooded animals who show little emotion whether they made $1million or lost $1million. If my guy acted like this on the demo account, imagine the commotion when trading with real money! I knew it would be a waste of time and capital to keep him, so I quickly let him go. He took it hard, sobbing as I told him I was doing him a favor, saving him from wasting blood, sweat, and tears on an impossible dream.

One week gone, and only four of my crack team remained! But I was still confident there was at least one great trader in the bunch. The math wizard and the chess champion seemed made for the business, but I was most excited about the prospects of the 18-year-old part-time high school student and full-time gaming prodigy. However, these high hopes were dampened when he started skipping work after just a couple of weeks. In hindsight, I should have fired him straight away. He was clearly a "piker" in Ben Affleck's vernacular. Instead, I pulled a move that isn't exactly straight from the Wall Street playbook, calling his mother to let her know that her boy was half-assing it. After a swift lecture from his parents, his attendance improved, but it wasn't exactly a slick ass move.

My main work with my reduced team was tutoring them to become hardcore scalpers. Any talk of fancy technical patterns or fundamental analysis was strictly forbidden; glitches and niches were the pillars of this training plan.

A good glitch or niche will only prove worthwhile if the trader is disciplined. This means cutting your losers, not overtrading, sticking to your strategies, and busting your ass to ensure you do everything needed to succeed. Being able to perform the excruciating act of sitting and waiting for a trade, or having the discipline to admit you are wrong time after time, are among the most formidable challenges any trader must conquer.

To help my rookies master these tasks and develop a sense of discipline, I made guidelines for them to follow. There were three rules for entering a trade: Having an exact price that they will cover their trade, having a reason why they will cover at that level, and having three reasons why they entered the trade. For instance, if they bought a stock at $10.05 in front of a significant technical support level at $10, their out should be $9.99, when the stock breaks support. Buying this stock in front of support would be one reason for entering the trade, with "The market going up" and "a big buyer in the order book at $10" potentially being the other two reasons.

These rules, combined with automated risk management parameters installed on their trading software, kept the crew on track. Things went smoothly the first year or so, and while none of the traders became consistently profitable, they generally made progress. Attrition was an inevitable part of the business, so a couple of traders left or were let go, including the young gaming prodigy, but I was always quick to replenish the office's stock.

Although running the business was hard work, and many of the tasks were tedious, there were facets that I enjoyed; coaching and recruiting gave me pleasure, and I loved being back in an office and trading as a group. The good atmosphere and camaraderie among the Cream Capital crew made all the hard work seem worth it, and the real payoff would be when the traders started to become profitable, which seemed just a matter of time since I sensed some traders were on the cusp of breaking through.

This camaraderie was a key to building a vibrant office and thus spawning profitable traders, so I sponsored "team building" trips to the local casino and visits to the numerous bars surrounding our office. I would use these bonding sessions to fill their heads with tales of legendary traders, epic trades, and visions of the luxurious lifestyle success afforded. The goal was to boost their confidence, but in hindsight, these stories may have caused them to wonder why their leader was taking the bus to go home rather than jumping in a fancy sports car to head to his mansion...

In reality, I was struggling to pay rent on my reasonably priced two-bedroom house in suburban Wroclaw. Despite being pleased with how the firm was shaping up, not surprisingly I was finding it difficult to focus on my own trading on top of all the additional responsibilities of running a firm.

The trading gods weren't doing me, or the firm, any favors either. I know this sounds like a broken record, but the first two years of the company's existence were marked by some of the least volatile periods in stock market history. Fortunately, even in this dead market and juggling my own trading with running the firm, there were always a couple of glitch strategies out there to tap into, enabling me to grind out enough each month to pay the bills—yet another testament to the power of the glitch! However, I was still always a bad month or one bad trade away from the abyss.

Not surprisingly, as the harsh market conditions persisted, the firm's traders also found the going tough. Most of them flirted with profitability—and those who didn't managed to keep their losses small; however, the software fees, office rent and bills, and numerous other costs took their toll on the company's limited financial resources. Of course, my original budget for the firm was overly optimistic, meaning that midway through its third year, in the summer of 2015, Cream Capital was fighting for its financial survival.

The market doldrums showed no signs of abating, and the wave of volatility meant to shower us all with cash was nowhere in sight. The company had only two months' worth of operating costs left in the bank, and I had to beg our landlord to let us use our rental deposit as rent for the month.

I felt guilty keeping the news of the dire state of the company from the traders, but I knew that if any of them made money, they would still get paid, and the company's share of the profits would prolong our existence. I also didn't want to cause any traders to adopt reckless "just fuck it" trading methodologies and risk putting us out of business altogether. Despite my worries, I wasn't ready to give up.

As bad as things were with the company, things were even more precarious regarding my own trading. Having been able to grind out just enough profits to keep my family and me afloat for the last couple of years, it seemed my luck was finally about to run out. In August, my own account was bone dry, and I was ready to accept defeat on all fronts. The plan was to disband the company at the end of the month and hold a fire sale of the company's computers and monitors so I could pay my bills.

As I was about to wave the white flag, trouble began to stir in the markets. 21st August was a big red day, and I sensed that a great wave of volatility might be approaching. The 24th of August brought panic in China, with the Chinese equity market selling off almost 10% overnight. Correspondently, the U.S markets were indicating a big gap down in the premarket session. As the official opening of the market approached, these indications continued to slip as fear gripped the markets. This sudden and shocking drop spooked everyone, sending buyers running for the hills. The ultra-sensitive trading bots were frightened too, scared perhaps that this could turn into a repeat of the 2010 flash crash debacle. Liquidity had evaporated—it is exactly what I had been waiting for!

Many of my favorite stocks indicated drops of 20% or more on their opening auctions (remember these auctions from the Tesla trade), which seemed way out of whack, considering the broad market indicated a drop of around 5%– these stocks were overreacting to the fear. Everything was happening fast, but I knew the play was to put out as many buy-limit orders at low and favorable prices on these familiar stocks indicated to open with huge discounts. If my orders got filled at these low prices on this auction, I would quickly sell once their prices had hopefully bounced back up and recalibrated with the broad market. It was a classic bottom-picking/lagging strategy, or even comparable to my favorite sports betting strategy back in college, the one where I picked point spreads that looked out of whack.

During the critical seconds right before the market opened, I scanned the market for these "glitching stocks" and maxed out what little capital I had left in my account, placing buy orders at what I thought were highly advantageous prices. The markets opened as usual at 9:30 a.m. U.S Eastern Time, but because of the intense action, the auction trades on these stocks were delayed while the exchanges matched up the orders.

A few minutes after the market had officially opened, volume and volatility in the market had surged, and some of my orders started to get executed. As soon as one of my buy orders got filled and transformed into an actual position, I would quickly sell, hoping for a quick profit as it jumped back up in line with the overall market, and also relieving myself of the risk of being at the mercy of this crazy market. Everything was happening so fast that I wasn't paying attention to my P&L total, just pounding my sell button and getting out of every stock I had bought as fast as possible.

After about five extremely intense minutes, my positions were all closed, the madness had ended, the dust had cleared, and my heart rate finally receded. After catching my breath, I glanced down at my profit total on my screen, and a juicy five-digit green figure greeted my wild eyes. I hadn't seen a number like that in a long time and I let out a huge scream!

My euphoria was briefly replaced by a sense of disappointment when I heard that some of the big dogs in the Texas office had made 6 or 7 figures–compared to my paltry 25k–but my ego quickly recalibrated once I remembered the dreadful state my trading account had been in just minutes earlier, and I went back to rejoicing this gift from the market gods.

This was the first "real action" they had ever seen, but that didn't stop a couple of the Cream crew from jumping into the madness. Limited experience, and capital, meant the profits were small, but it was still enough to throw the firm a lifeline for a couple more months. That was a huge relief and a positive sign for their trading; It took guts to jump into the chaos, and skill to come out with profits. I was also proud of myself for getting them to a place where they could take advantage of such a situation.

I had hoped that this wave of volatility was just the start of a storm, but sadly, the market calmed down within days. When the market doldrums returned, it didn't take long for me and the firm to drain our windfall. By early 2016, the firm was down to 3 traders and back on life support. I had returned to my monthly pitch battles with the markets, fighting tooth and nail to support my family.

We fought hard, but the markets ultimately prevailed, and the firm was bankrupt by the summer of 2016. Accepting defeat came with the relief that I would no longer have the stress of running a firm and could focus on my own personal battle for fiscal survival.

When I broke the news to the remaining two traders, I told them I was doing them a favor and that their considerable skills were wasted in this industry and at this firm. One of them agreed, but the other, my most recent hire, a confident and gifted 20-year-old named Denis, who had achieved the almost impossible feat of making money in his first month, wanted to stay on. He wasn't ready to accept defeat, and, knowing he had tons of potential, we agreed that he would trade remotely and be kept on a tight leash.

Despite the faint hope that Denis would resurrect the firm, I accepted that the business had ultimately failed. Apart from feeling guilty about losing John and Mike's investment, and the extreme pressure involved towards the end, I have mainly fond memories of Cream Capital Group. It was a mistake undertaking this business with so little capital and trying to do everything myself, but I still believe if we had market conditions similar to 2008 or 2020, the business and its traders would have thrived.

A couple of the ex-Cream Capital traders did end up thriving in the trading world at more professional outfits, including one ex-trader who made it to the top of the profession, working at one of the most prestigious firms in the world. As you will read later in the book, a couple of the guys went in a different direction from trading, starting businesses, and then kindly, and somewhat stupidly, turned the tables and offered their old boss a job. The rest of the members of the old crew I keep in touch with seem to be doing well in their chosen professions.

Unlike those traders, I had no escape route. My lack of a backup plan left me trading out my spare bedroom and battling both the market and my own demons. Feeling exhausted and helpless, I started to exhibit some of those toxic habits that I talked about earlier. My back was firmly against the wall, and I started to get addicted to the euphoria and relief that came from the wins in this intense battle for survival. I was running on adrenaline and trading emotionally, in a manner quite opposite to how the successful trader operates.

I was more compulsive gambler than trader. I would lock myself in this bedroom and trade for hours, not following any plan, just fighting back and forth with the market. It was a joyless cycle, with every loss stinging like hell and the thrill of the win becoming duller by the day.

By late 2016, Denis had moved on, and that little light at the end of the tunnel was finally vanquished. Consumed with thoughts about trading, money, and survival, I barely slept. My toxic daily trading/gambling battles were now fueled more and more by my old diet of alcohol, weed, and junk food. Considering the harshness of the market and the fragility of my mental and physical condition, it was a miracle I was still standing. I must have pressed on through a survival instinct and a need to support my family—although, by this time, it was sadly only financial support that I was really offering.

The destructive cycle continued through the remainder of 2016, with me in a battered state. I was badly beaten but not ready to surrender, always on the edge of insolvency but still swinging away. As 2017 approached, my profits had dried up, and my account was running on empty. The markets had finally gotten the best of me; I was barely standing, clinging to the ropes. That's when the final knockout blow landed, but it didn't come from the markets. Ania let me know that she wanted a divorce and wanted me out of the house.

I was floored again. But this time, it was even harder than in the past, I was in a feeble state and it felt like it would be near-impossible to drag myself back to my feet. 2017 arrived with me about to turn 40, dead broke, and homeless in a foreign land. Happy New Year!

14.
Capitulation:
ICOohhh!

Capitulation—which I talked about a little in an earlier chapter—is the point when things get so bad that investors throw in the towel and sell. It is said that before a beaten-down asset reverses its trajectory, it must capitulate and shake out the "weak hands". Capitulation isn't typically a term we use outside of finance, but it seems a perfect word to describe my state in early 2017. I was so beaten down that Ania decided to cut her loser.

Ania was hardly a "weak hand", the punch she delivered was mighty painful, but also somewhat expected. Ania had tired of dealing with my downward trajectory, basically throwing in the towel on our marriage when the company disbanded. It was tough to blame her for her decision to leave me, but it still left me feeling betrayed, hurt, and guilty.

I soon realized that divorce was the best remedy for our toxic relationship and was also the impetus I needed (once again) to make me try and get out of a self-destructive downward spiral. I regretted that it had taken another divorce to set me straight, especially as the dissolution of this marriage came with much more collateral damage.

Everything was darker; I was older, with no money and no home, and most importantly, there were two precious girls caught in the middle. I felt truly ashamed of myself for my behavior over the last year and for the type of father and man I had become.

It was quite a hole I had dug myself into, and it would be a big challenge to climb out, but I was determined to fight and turn things around. The first step was finding a place to live.

Although rents are reasonably cheap in Poland, finding a place to live while I was dead broke was going to be a challenge. My consoling father must have had some bottom-picker in him because he agreed to step in and support his capitulated son. We concocted a plan in which he and his new wife would save me from the streets by moving to Poland and sharing an apartment with me, which he would graciously pay for. My dad and I had always had somewhat of a turbulent relationship, and I didn't really have any relationship with his new wife, so it was a nice gesture for them to come to my rescue. It was also a nice opportunity for them as they had been restless living in Texas, and both craved a cooler climate and the European lifestyle. My dad's wife also wanted to be closer to her mother, who lived in Ukraine. Poland isn't the most common destination for retirees (it's not exactly Florida), but it met their needs.

I found us a small two-bedroom apartment not far from Ania and my girls, and—in the spring of 2017, after a welcome twenty-year break—I moved back in with my dad. It was a surreal scene; my retired English dad and his Ukrainian wife sharing a small apartment with their destitute 40-year-old son in the middle of Poland. It was a big blow to my ego. I was like Benjamin Button; everything in my life was happening in the wrong chronological order. I was getting poorer with age, becoming less secure in life, and now I was back to living with my dad.

Now with a roof over my head, the next step was finding a job. I dusted off my resume once again and added my Cream Capital gig, thinking that running a firm and my CEO title would finally grab some attention. Of course, I didn't mention that I was a failed and bankrupt CEO, I was just "looking for new opportunities".

A big European bank, which had a large office in Wroclaw, took the bait, offering me an interview for a Finance Manager position. I realized I was way out of my depth just minutes into the interview when the person across the table from me started talking in a different language. It wasn't Polish, but some weird corporate speak. My "looking for new opportunities" line was the extent of my corporate-speak vocabulary, so the interview was a disaster. Now I would need to do my own "thinking outside the box", "pivot", and find the best fit for my "core competencies".

This meant "leveraging" the one skill I possessed that had some value in Poland: my relative mastery of my mother tongue. Teaching English isn't a core competency of mine, but I approached language schools because I was desperate and didn't have any other options. A few years earlier, I wouldn't have imagined getting myself in a position where I would be begging for a $10/hour part-time job, but that was the dire situation I was in.

I ended up begging because I performed dreadfully in the interview... again. In the end, my painful-sounding but honest plea of "I'm desperately trying to support my daughters" worked, and I got the gig. The plan was to work part-time, teaching English to corporate workers at a local office, and juggle this with the uphill task of replenishing my meager trading account and getting my trading career back on track.

My Polish was awful, but I soon found out that my mastery of English wasn't that good either. I realized that I didn't know an adjective from an adverb when I was simply given a course book and a list of student names, along with a warning not to fuck up. There was no training program or rousing Ben Affleck-style speech.

My new job was a refreshing change from trading, and I enjoyed it. It had been almost 20 years since I had a real job (if you want to describe my broker job as "real"), so it was interesting to see how normal civilians went about their jobs and lives. It was quite shocking to see that these workers—who I might once have considered slaves to faceless corporations—actually enjoyed their non-exhilarating jobs. It made sense since they felt part of a team, generally enjoyed their tasks, and, most importantly, were paid regularly each month. Security like that means never having to go through the hell I went through. Combine that with complimentary coffee and plenty of office parties, and it's no wonder they were so happy.

The teaching part wasn't as stressful as I imagined. A typical lesson involved a leisurely chat about what we did at the weekend or maybe reading and discussing an article about a topic I was interested in, like sports, politics, crypto, or finance. Most students just wanted to practice their conversation skills with a native speaker. I even served as a quasi-therapist to some who would just tell me about their problems.

I was also receiving therapeutic benefits. Meeting people and having a conversation worked wonders after those torturous months of being locked up in my bedroom office. It was good to try something new, and the job served as a welcome distraction from my troubles. Teaching a handful of lessons a week at $10 a pop didn't make for an excellent reserve parachute, but the positive side effects from the job were benefitting my trading, making my teaching a great investment.

I had taken other steps to improve my life in general: making an effort to exercise, eat better, drink less, make new friends, spend time doing hobbies, and be a better father. Of course, all of this made me happier and healthier, which made me a better trader. We can talk about trading styles, strategies, and market conditions all day long, but it all means nothing if the trader's head isn't on straight.

One of my favorite things about trading is that, typically, the happier you are, the better you trade—thus making it more likely you will make money. What a great job to have; one in which more happiness usually equals more cash! Following this logic, spending money on things that make you happy is an excellent investment. I even have the data to back this up; my profits always tend to spike after traveling.

The end of the last chapter is a great example of the flip side of this happiness equation; dark moods equate to poor trading performance, typically leading to losses. With an unhealthy mindset, the markets will show little compassion, only causing more pain and suffering. If you are not feeling right mentally, the best course of action is to stay well away.

Despite having little money to "invest" in my happiness, it finally felt like my head was back on straight. My toxic trading habits disappeared, and with a structured trading plan and some discipline, my trading seemed to be back on track. Part of this new trading plan was a new niche I had carved out, focusing on trading the premarket session, which suited my style. As I mentioned earlier, the premarket session is slower, with less volume and fewer algos; perfect for a slow and aging trader who relies on tape reading and instincts.

My new niche revolved around scalping a small sub-sector of stocks in which I had found some repeating patterns and readable order books. My strategies were only to be traded in the calm premarket session and only for the hour before the market officially opened, a textbook example of a niche. Unfortunately, my strategies weren't scalable, and since they only took up only five hours of my time a week, another problem was staying disciplined and avoiding trading when there was no edge for me.

Overtrading has always been my Achilles heel. Even after over 20 years in the business, I still find it excruciating to sit in front of my computer and fight the temptation to trade unnecessarily. It is a crippling affliction, considering the vast majority of the time trading should be spent watching, searching, and stalking trades. I have tried everything short of tying my hands behind my back to remedy the problem. I'm not the only one who suffers, overtrading is a bad habit for nearly all traders—only the best are able to master the skill of just sitting and waiting.

For me, the only fail-safe cure is turning my trading software off and physically separating myself from my computer. Sadly, the temptation is sometimes so strong that I find it best to schedule "distractions" to keep me away from trading. Taking Polish lessons, going to the gym, and spending time with my daughters are not only productive ways to spend my time, but when scheduled correctly, they can also save me a lot of heartache and cash. For experienced traders (new traders need to be in front of the screens as much as possible) suffering from a similar case of this affliction, I would prescribe a similar regimen of distancing yourself from the tools of the trade.

It was imperative to stay disciplined in early 2018, as trading remained extremely challenging. Fortunately, this new niche of mine was suited for a low-volatility market, allowing me to pull out some small but consistent profits. I was finally following my own advice of having a method to grind out some profits in a dull market, which was a positive step, but I still longed for volatility. It had been ten long years since the madness of 2008/2009, and my six-figure months now seemed like nothing more than pipe dreams.

With no end to the volatility drought in sight, I had to do things the hard way. I was grinding out profits, but the bulk of these scraps and my meager teaching salary went straight to Ania or to paying off debt. I owned nothing but a beat-up car. It was a shock to my system to be now measuring my wealth by cartridges of razor blades and whether my petrol tank was full—this is what it now meant to be long steel or oil. On top of all this, I was still living with my dad!

Although grateful for their help, being cooped up with my dad and his wife in a small apartment was trying. It didn't take long for the mood to turn sour and—after six months of edginess and arguing—my dad decided that Poland wasn't the place for them.

I had my freedom again and took over the lease on the apartment, even though it would be a struggle to pay rent. I was making progress with my trading, but as I said earlier, new strategies take time to perfect, so I couldn't count on consistent trading income yet. Knowing It would be a constant battle to pay rent, bills, and my other expenses from my trading income and teaching salary, I knew I had to look for a side hustle.

A logical place to look was at the cryptocurrency markets. While volatility in equity markets sat dormant in 2017, things were wild in the cryptocurrency markets. Bitcoin had just gone from $800 to $20,000 in a year! Of course, I had missed that whole move, but I knew there must be opportunities with all of this volatility.

I didn't have the capital or the time to carefully study these markets and develop strategies; I was looking for a get-rich-quick type of deal. If I heard a rookie trader utter these words, I would slap them upside their head, but I was permitted to go this route because I was experienced enough to know exactly what I was looking for. And I was desperate.

I was looking for the holy grail of glitches—a golden arbitrage strategy. I knew there were arbitrage opportunities in these untamed and relatively bot-free crypto markets; I had seen it with my own eyes. Sadly, the inter-exchange arbitrage Bitcoin opportunity I mentioned in chapter 3 had been discovered by the masses by the beginning of 2018. The crowd, and the bots, had narrowed the price difference between the exchanges, sucking out the edge from this once bountiful strategy. Although I was late to the party, it still gave me hope that other similar strategies were waiting to be discovered.

To find this sacred strategy, I went to places even wilder and more chaotic than the crypto markets: YouTube and Twitter. Yes, this seems like another bout of hypocrisy after all of my jibes; however, while I still stress caution about using these platforms for trading education, I do think there is valuable content available for those who know how to filter through all the garbage. Thankfully, sifting through bullshit is one skill I have developed over the years working in finance.

I knew the odds of finding anyone sharing valuable secrets were long, but I typed "crypto arbitrage" into YouTube and went to work. After a few days of searching and listening to countless idiots spout nonsense, I unearthed a video from a young man named Hien. He was the leader of what he called his "wolfpack", a group that bonded over trading crypto and selling specialized tungsten rings. Despite that odd combination—and the fact that this video had only a couple of dozen views and looked like it was filmed in his garage—it piqued my interest. He talked of an ICO (Initial Coin Offering) arbitrage opportunity. The more I listened, the more I realized the guy was talking some sense; he was explaining a legitimate arbitrage strategy.

I won't fully explain this strategy because it's fairly complicated and technical (I have included a link at the end of the book to the actual YouTube video where he explains the strategy), but it revolved around an ICO (crypto's version of an IPO) auction that took place every 23 hours for about six months. Since we were into about the third month of the ICO, I was able to back-test this wolfpack strategy, and my results showed that it was golden! It seemed to have plenty of edge and was hidden from the masses. I was ecstatic about my findings, but to execute this strategy, I needed Ethereum tokens as leverage.

John came to the rescue, letting me borrow a big chunk of his personal holdings of Ethereum.

I began trading this new strategy at the beginning of 2018. It was a totally different trading process to what I was used to, being much more complicated and with even less room for error. The whole process for the trade usually took about 30 minutes and involved not only trading the coins but shuffling them back and forth from my crypto wallet to this auction, and then to the exchange. When I'm equity trading, one little slip on the keys can mean losing a sizable chunk of cash, but a one-digit error in an address during any part of this complicated crypto strategy would have meant I (or, rather, John) lost everything.

I was initially disappointed with my results, but it didn't take long for the profits to start rolling in. The auctions lasted only a couple more months, so once I gained confidence in the strategy, I kept upping my trading size. All my profits were in this Ethereum token, and out of necessity, as soon as I made any profits, I would quickly exchange the Ethereum into dollars. It turned out to be a wise decision not to become a HODL; as soon as I started trading this strategy, the crypto markets crashed, and the value of this Ethereum token went from $1400 to $400 in a few months. It also meant my bottom-picking tendencies would have meant I would have gotten cut to pieces by the falling knives if I had stepped into this market with anything other than a glitch strategy.

Since this auction happened every 23 hours, I traded at all types of unusual times and in strange places. I remember the many times I had to set my alarm for the middle of the night and then attempt to execute this complicated strategy while still half-asleep. Other times I found myself doing it on a bus or tram on the way to my teaching job. Occasionally, I would find a little corner in the corporate office between my lessons to quickly punch out some profits.

I even took a break from a wedding I attended to attempt this trade. I say attempt, because I soon realized how drunk I was and prudently decided that hitting the dancefloor would be a smarter alternative.

Fortunately, and perhaps miraculously, I always sent these tokens to the correct address. When the strategy ended, I had a nice little haul of $30,000, which saved my ass. Thanks to the Hien and the Wolfpack, I could now comfortably pay my rent and bills, save a little, and even have a little fun on the side.

Relieved and grateful, I wrote an email to Hien thanking him, and tried to explain that by sharing this video, he was handing out free money to anyone who listened and happened to know the value of a good arbitrage strategy. I assumed he was oblivious to his kindness, as there is never any benefit to randomly sharing an arbitrage strategy; crowds only hurt these magical cash-making miracles. Who knows, maybe he was just a kindhearted soul. I have no idea what his motivation was because he never answered my email. He probably thought, "I just saved this guy's ass, the least he could do is buy one of my tungsten rings!"

15.

Cryptocurrency: Executive Decision

The legendary Hien opened my eyes to the opportunities in the world of crypto and its markets. It was a fantastic playground full of obscene volatility and was a goldmine for arbitrage opportunities. Cryptocurrency itself revolved around revolutionary technology and was the home to some of the brightest, most colorful, and sometimes sketchiest characters on the face of the planet. I was intrigued and excited about all the potential opportunities. I just thought these opportunities would be on the trading side of things, rather than becoming one of those sketchy crypto characters.

Putting my initial crypto windfall in the bank and building a small safety net would have been the wise thing to do. However, I used a decent chunk to do some traveling, reasoning that I was investing a little happiness (which would make me a better trader) and giving myself a little needed relief from the pressures of an ongoing messy divorce.

Traveling positively influences my trading, but it turns out that my actual trading improves on the road. When I travel, I sometimes take my laptop to lift a little of the guilt of spending the money (and also to keep me away from casinos in case I need a dopamine hit). However, I was shocked when I went over my trading data and realized that my daily P&L was twice as high when I traded while traveling (this data doesn't include 2020, because in that type of market you need speed and lots of monitor space, so trading from your regular battle station is imperative).

It's necessary to take some breaks in which you're entirely free from the grips of the markets; these trading-free breaks should be part of every trader's plan to combat the stress and pressure of the job. As I travel excessively, it makes sense for me to sometimes pack my laptop and sacrifice the hour each day it typically takes to execute my strategies. Being able to trade remotely is one of the great benefits of this job; you can do this job anywhere in the world with a decent internet connection. Of course, trading on holiday can backfire; a bad trading day is never pleasant, and losing has an even more wicked bite when it spoils a holiday. On the flip side, it's pretty sweet to make a few thousand dollars while chilling on the beach in the Mediterranean.

"Why are the results better?" you may ask. I hypothesize that it's because I'm more relaxed while on holiday, creating a better mindset for trading. I also tend to trade with more discipline, not pushing it as much. Also, once the time window for my strategy passes, I am a lot less likely to be undisciplined and keep trading as the beach, pool, mountains, or town await. I suggest every trader delve into their own trading data and see what environment, time periods, and even what days of the week produce their best results. If the results are poor while traveling, then that is a great excuse to keep that laptop in the bag and just enjoy your travels instead.

My traveling and improved mindset shouldn't get all the credit for my improved trading results; it was natural that the more I traded my new niche strategies, the better my feel and execution became. That's the beauty of having a niche! As my confidence grew, my profits grew. Which made my confidence grow even more, and my results in turn... It's a blissful cycle that keeps repeating itself!

Unfortunately, there is a flip side to this cycle; low confidence creates poor performance, which causes poor results—which can also become a feedback loop. It is a cruel cycle and easy to get sucked into, and typically spells doom for a trading career. As you have read, I had taken a couple of rides in this nasty and turbulent cycle, fortunately getting spat out just in time, but not before causing plenty of damage to both my P&L and my mental condition.

The key to avoiding a downward spiral is awareness. The trader must realize they are getting sucked in and then take the right steps, which usually means stepping away before things get out of control. On the other side of things, while confidence is generally a good thing, too much confidence can also be an extremely costly affliction—just as was for those "lottery winning" rookies from 2008. Overconfidence can quickly turn into recklessness. The trader needs to be aware when they are starting to push too hard, and ease off the throttle.

I wasn't at the stage where I had to worry about overconfidence, but I was at least confident enough in my trading to quit my English teaching job. The time was right. The novelty had faded, and my bosses started complaining about my lack of lesson planning. I thought it would be better to quit and save myself the embarrassment of getting fired.

It also seemed quite silly to have this job since I would sometimes leave the school, go home and trade, and then make (or sometimes lose) the equivalent of six months teaching salary in a few seconds. I was acting like my old student Jeremy Liu.

That situation was a classic example of a nasty side effect of trading: the skewing of the value of money. Traders sometimes fall into that trap of knowing the price of every stock but the value of nothing. Your mind becomes warped by money when one click of a mouse can pay for a new home; it suddenly seems futile to make an effort to save a few bucks while shopping. My mom would be devastated to hear me talk like that, so for the sake of fiscal responsibility and my own sanity, I still hit the sales racks and try to separate my P&L from real-world money.

Back in 2018, I wasn't paying off a mortgage in a single stroke anyway. The continuing volatility drought was driving all of us traders insane and prompting people to once again say that "Day trading is dead!" Traders were dropping like flies, John and Mike struggled, and that Texas office was basically deserted. Fortunately, my premarket niche kept me going... but it meant I had a lot of free time on my hands. I decided to use this time to write a book about my experiences while trading, not as an obituary to the profession but as an inspiration and a warning to others who might be interested in getting started.

I just got into a decent flow of writing and trading, finding a nice balance in my life after so much upheaval. And then a call from an ex-Cream Capital trader threw everything out of equilibrium.

I had kept in touch with most of the Cream crew, and it seemed they all were doing well—in fact, the company's demise seemed like a blessing. Kamil, one of the ex-traders, had settled down in his small hometown and was running his family's grocery store business, so I was a little surprised when he called me and informed me that he was getting involved in the world of crypto startups. I was even more surprised when Kamil asked me if I would be interested in becoming CEO of a sports-related crypto startup that he was investing in. I still dreamed of receiving a nice steady paycheck—and a job with crypto, sports, and CEO in the title covered all my loves. So, even though I was both a little skeptical and quite unqualified, I was certainly interested!

I met Kamil, and the money man behind the project, Adam. They explained to me, in an extremely delicate manner, that they were looking for a "businessman" with an English-sounding name and face to head their project. It seemed David Hale, CEO, sounded much more legitimate than, say, Pawel Kowalski, CEO, in the Western-centric world of crypto. I guess it wasn't a shock that my name and non-Slavic looks were of more importance than my actual business pedigree, considering my actual business pedigree.

Since Adam would still be running things, it was more of a "puppet CEO" role, making me worried that I would be selling out by taking the job. The Wu-Tang Clan and my other favorite rappers always warned about "keeping it real", but I turned my back on my heroes and their creed after being told of the generous salary and the chance to make millions if the project succeeded. I was determined to land this job, putting on my best CEO act during our brief conversation about the specifics of the job. After our discussion, we moved to a sketchy college nightclub, where the job interview continued till 3 in the morning.

It seemed they were looking for a bad dancer who could down shots of vodka as the face of the company, because when I woke the following day, a message that they wanted me to be their CEO greeted me and my hangover. Sell out or not, I was excited! I couldn't wait to meet interesting people, learn the crypto business, and make lots of cash. We agreed that I would move to Tychy, Poland, and start as soon as possible.

In hindsight, red flags were raised from the start because not only was this crypto company hiring a part-time English teacher as its CEO, but the firm was also headquartered in Tychy. I hate to compare Tychy and Grays because of my love for Grays, but Tychy would be a prime candidate for "Poland's capital of misery." It is an example of a post-war socialist planning policy gone awry. This small industrial city sits in the heart of the Polish coal mining region and is packed with ugly Communist-era apartment buildings and smokey factories. Not surprisingly, it has some of the worst air quality in the world. All of this makes it an extremely unusual place to launch a crypto startup.

Another red flag was raised when I handed my lawyer a copy of the badly written contract that I was finally given after continued pleading. His first words were, "You sure you want your face on this project?" I had no reputation for ruining, so I put pen to paper.

Upon my arrival in Tychy in the late summer of 2018, Adam gave me a tour and did his best to sell me on the city and the project. I met some of the other people involved; they were all nice enough, but I was uncertain about their qualifications to launch a cryptocurrency token with any success. In fact, it seemed this crypto business was the offshoot of a real estate company that focused on building retirement homes. It was a strange crossover.

The more I heard, the more I knew everyone was out of their depth, including myself. The suspicion that this was some type of elaborate scam began to creep into my mind. I might have even preferred to be head of some well-run criminal enterprise than the head of a poorly run crypto startup destined to fail. I didn't dare to ask them straight up if this was a scam; I thought they might not want to divulge right away if it was shady, and if it wasn't, they would be deeply offended by the question.

It's hard for me to explain exactly what this project was because I didn't fully understand, and still honestly don't. It called itself a "community-driven digital environment empowering sports fans." The idea was to build an app, launch an ICO, and cash in on this crypto craze, or what was soon to be the crypto bubble (when companies like this one emerge, it is always a good indication that the bubble is about to pop).

Although never shown any financial numbers, the more I saw and heard, the more I worried. I knew I hadn't been hired to perform a traditional CEO role, but by my third day, I couldn't hold my tongue any longer. I sat down with the key stakeholders and–with the help of a translator and in the most gentle manner possible–proposed ending the venture. I thought it was destined to fail and believed that a good alternative would be to use this cash to invest directly into cryptocurrency, with me as the portfolio manager. It might not have been exactly what they wanted to hear from their new CEO on his third day, but they didn't seem that bothered and assured me they wanted to go full speed ahead with their project.

After accepting their answer and coming to peace with the fact that I was either CEO of a criminal enterprise or an inept semi-legitimate business, I decided to just go with the flow and enjoy the adventure. The first couple of months were spent cruising around Poland, attending business meetings which usually turned into vodka-fueled, all-night parties. When not on the road, I lived in a surreal 70s-disco-themed motel in the Polish countryside outside of Tychy. The shag carpeting must have brought me luck because I was on fire on the local dating scene; my CEO title and "Texan" blazed across my Tinder dating profile worked wonders in that part of the world. This sketchy crypto world was turning out to be a blast!

Sadly, it didn't take long before the good times ended, and things started to sour. One cause of my disenchantment was being asked to make promotional videos. It wasn't an unreasonable request, but the introvert in me dreaded making these cheesy ads for the business. Moreover, the semi-respectable businessman, hidden deep inside me, suddenly didn't want my face on the project!

I went ahead and made them, and the main damage caused was the hazing from my friends who got hold of these cringe-worthy films. It's something they still hit me with today!

These videos weren't the only source of embarrassment; our meetings with investors also became a source of humiliation. Somehow, we managed to schedule a few meetings with real crypto people or real investors, and each time we were embarrassingly outgunned. I could see the looks of disgust on their faces as we wasted their valuable time, attempting feebly to sell our shitty product with an even worse sales pitch. Sometimes we were shown a sense of pity, which I found particularly painful. Usually, the meetings were just cut short with a mild-mannered Polish version of "get the fuck outta here!"

I found it even more soul-destroying when I was told to start pitching our product to less sophisticated investors. I hoped that most of these "unsophisticated investors" were smart enough to tell us to hit the road, but I didn't want any part of this shady game. I still had nightmares of my old broker job and being told to cold call unsuspecting grandmothers, but this was 100 times worse. Offering an unsuitable and underperforming mutual fund is bad, but pitching a crypto token that I was almost certain would be worthless was bordering on criminal behavior.

Living in Tychy was also getting old. The four-hour train trip to see my daughters on the weekends was tiresome. I missed them and wanted to go back "home" to Wroclaw. The fact that the crypto bubble had popped made my decision to quit a no-brainer. Even If this was indeed a legitimate business, the chances of it succeeding now went from very slim to none.

After about five months on the job, I packed my bags and headed home for good at Christmas 2018. I still wasn't sure if I had just resigned as the CEO of a doomed crypto startup or as the leader of a doomed criminal enterprise. It took a fight to get my name and "face" erased from the promotional material and an even bigger battle to get my last paycheck, but I had no regrets.

Shockingly, someone was impressed by my CEO tenure because I had a job waiting for me when I returned to Wroclaw. Denis, Cream Capital's last trader, had started a website-building business and offered me a Global Sales

Manager position at his startup. It seemed a little strange to go from being his boss to him becoming my 22-year-old boss, but I was willing to swallow what was left of my pride. I knew that great things awaited Denis; the guy was smart, driven, and full of swagger. It seemed a great idea to get the stink of my last job off me by attaching myself to this winner and his promising business.

Denis' business, Bejamas, was the polar opposite of what I had just come from; it was a well-led, legitimate business. Denis taught me the ropes, and then it was up to me to hustle and make some sales. I was finally working for a skilled professional and selling a quality product, but it didn't take too many months of spam messaging LinkedIn contacts to realize that sales isn't a "core competency" of mine.

In all honesty, it didn't seem that it mattered what I was doing; working for someone and doing anything other than trading seemed impossible for me. Other jobs lacked the thrill of trading and just seemed boring. Both my good and bad experiences in the so-called real world only made me keener to get back to trading full time. I missed the excitement, independence, freedom, and profit potential.

Yes, I had lost more than a few battles with this profession of mine, resulting in plenty of dark times, but the wounds were healing, and the love was returning. It's almost impossible to remain completely unscathed in this ruthless profession. Still, with the right mindset and a winning trading plan, the trader holds the advantage over the market.

It all sounds so simple, and I was confident of my mental state and my hard-won trading experience, so I had no doubt I could conquer the markets. Considering the generally harsh trading conditions of the previous decade, it would be an uphill struggle, but I still had some faint hope that the long-awaited volatility wave would finally come in and drench me with riches.

My brief and fairly fruitless foray into the civilian world was over. I went back to being a full-time professional trader. To quote Inspectah Deck's verse from C.R.E.A.M, I was now "A man with a dream with plans to make cream."

16.
A Return to Trading: Volatility to the Rescue

If I were going to pick a "hero" of this book, then volatility is the thing that sometimes swoops in to save the day and change my own trading fortunes. Despite mentioning it time and time again, our "hero" only makes fleeting appearances...so far.

As we know by now, volatility is a godsend for traders, but typically spells doom for the rest of the population. Hardly a savior, it's more of a Grim Reaper or antihero at best. Its appearance in 2008 coincided with massive losses in wealth and jobs for the general public. So, it feels wrong to be talking about volatility making a heroic return and providing a "happy ending" to this book.

You know what is coming next...

While this final chapter outlines a change in my personal fortunes, the "good times" for traders always leave something of a bitter taste in the mouth. It's impossible for any trader to call it a happy ending when the change in our own personal fortunes is brought about by a global pandemic that kills millions or a brutal and senseless war that is happening right on my own doorstep. That is the state of the world as I write this in late-2022.

Back in mid-2019, volatility was nowhere to be seen when I snipped the lifeline Denis had thrown me and set sail, once again navigating the tranquil waters of the equity markets full-time. These were peaceful and prosperous times. The Nasdaq and S&P were on track for a whopping 30-plus percent yearly return, which was great for buy-and-hold investors but not so good for bottom picking day traders like myself.

Regardless, I had been consistently profitable for the last couple of years and had proven to myself that I had the strategies and discipline to bring in enough cash each month to live a comfortable life in Poland. Fortunately, that doesn't take much, as a modest trading income enables one to live like a king in Central Eastern Europe. In fact, Wroclaw, and Poland in general, is a great place to trade from. Not only is it affordable and the Poles nice people, but it also sits in a friendly time zone for trading U.S markets and is a perfect place from which to travel.

Despite my consistency, my profits were small, so I was still only one bad month, or one disastrous trade from annihilation. I tried to bury that thought in my mind, and instead concentrate on the positives. Although I didn't have fancy cars or mansions, or even a sturdy safety net, I had freedom and independence, which I consider the greatest prize for being a profitable trader.

I was lucky to have my consistent pre-market strategy, which afforded me my rosy outlook on things. The mood was much darker in Austin, where day trading really did seem on its last legs. These were Texas gunslingers, used to blasting six-figure trading months, and they weren't willing to settle for grinding out paltry four-figure months like I was. Mike had decided by then that there was more edge in playing poker professionally than trading. Many at the Austin office smartly switched to automated trading, and others quit. The office was beginning to resemble a ghost town, and it seemed to be on the cusp of losing another grizzled veteran.

Like most traders, John thrived in the volatile markets and struggled in the slow times. However, his swings were even more extreme than most, and since it had been over ten years since we had real sustained volatility, he was in bad shape, with his trading account running on fumes. Not only was he facing a separation from trading, but he was also going through a divorce from his wife. There were, of course, other variables, but it's another painful reminder of the damage that this oftentimes toxic profession can cause.

2020 started off with John half-heartedly searching for a job, and the markets dead, just as they had been for the vast majority of the previous ten years. Although I was in the midst of the longest streak of profitable months in my career, I was also longing for a big payday that would ease my worries and take the pressure off the struggle of grinding out small profits.

It was a perfect environment for one of my more destructive habits to rear its head. When I'm restless, and in search of a big payday, instead of going with the flow, I have the propensity to veer from my training plan and try to predict (guess) which direction the markets are going. To put this in the most simple terms, I stop trading and start gambling.

This self-sabotaging habit has cost me hundreds of thousands of dollars over the years, and I'm not the only one suffering from this costly affliction, it seems most day traders are hell-bent on speculating. For the masses it makes sense, it is the easy path, and this is what they are fed on Twitter and from their "gurus", but I know better, I know my job is to mechanically execute a strategy with an edge, not to predict or guess. I guess deep down I still crave that rush, or maybe it's an ego thing; I want to be the celebrity hedge fund manager on CNBC receiving adulation for timing the market perfectly. It just seems more glamorous and exciting than perfectly executing a scalping trade for a 50-cent profit.

Over the prior couple of years, I controlled my gambling urges and finally got my trading ego in check, accepting that it's better to ignore the market as a whole and just stick to my strategies. Watching the market only causes biases for me. Forecasting the markets is also something I'm not qualified for; that's the job of the Wall Street Hedge Funds and big money managers like Warren Buffett—and by looking at their returns, it seemed they struggled at that task despite all of their resources. If they struggle, what hope does a day trader working out of his bedroom in Poland have?

The last 20 years had confirmed that I was awful at predicting the market. My contrarian nature meant I had been bearish for this whole bull market, but this still didn't stop me from trying to jump in and short the top of the market in early 2020. The temptation was too strong; I was certain this time (just like I had been certain countless other times in the last ten years) that this was the top.

Of course, I was wrong. The markets didn't care about escalating tensions between the U.S and Iran, or any other bearish news, instead they screamed to new highs and burned me once again. It seemed nothing could stop this bull market.

That's when we started hearing chatter about a pandemic in China. In early February, the talk loudened, and my Twitter feed began to fill with scary videos of zombie cruise ships stuck at sea with hundreds of sick passengers. A deadly global pandemic seemed like it could be something that might scare investors, but—just like every other threat of the previous decade—the market initially shrugged it off.

By late February, the virus rapidly spread worldwide, and the chatter turned to screams. The markets finally got spooked too, and the VIX popped. The panic spread, and within days the volatility index had exploded above 50—a level not seen since 2008. As the markets blew through support levels, I quickly realized this was the real deal. This was the volatility tsunami we had been waiting for through all these long and quiet years in the doldrums.

I was used to trading an hour a day in the calmest market conditions, so all this market madness shocked my system. I wasn't mentally or physically prepared. It was as if I was a recreational basketball player suddenly being catapulted into the NBA finals. I was unprepared physically, mentally, and even technically. Trading out of my bedroom with an outdated computer and a sluggish internet connection meant I was playing the NBA finals in Chuck Taylors instead of Air Jordans.

This antiquated trading setup had sufficed during the quiet markets, but now it couldn't handle the explosion of quotes and data that needed to be processed. The haunting memories of missing out on the big profits of 2008 flashed through my head. I thought about hopping on a flight to Texas to trade in that office, but it seemed too risky. Even getting there presented a challenge during the global panic and disruption to flights… and who knows how long I might be stuck there if I did make it to Texas.

Luckily, I had just started dating a nice woman whose tiny apartment had an ultra-fast internet connection. So, after only a few weeks of dating, I begged her to let me move in and trade from there. The poor girl didn't know what had hit her when I showed up with all my gear and set up shop. With my huge workstation taking up about half of the space, there was barely enough room to move inside the apartment. Unfortunately, this was a time when interior space was an especially hot commodity, considering we were on full COVID lockdown.

It was the ultimate test for our budding relationship, and the crazy markets were the ultimate test for my rusty trading skills. I was up for the challenge–regarding the trading part, at least–and ready to ride this giant wave of volatility that had finally landed. It was quite a swell–the wildest market since 2008–so I had to quickly reset my whole trading mindset and adjust my trading plan accordingly. Unfortunately, I didn't have a massive buffer in my trading account, so I couldn't be over-aggressive. If I made one false move I would be flattened under the wave and drowning in losses.

It only took me a couple of days to cushion my account, so I quickly became more and more aggressive, adding to my "size". That also meant mentally adjusting to those bigger swings in my P&L. Going from $100 losing trades to $10,000 losing trades in a couple of days definitely fucks with your mind.

Switching strategies was another necessity since the market volatility had killed my pre-market niche strategy (but this was fine because that strategy had only a limited upside, and I needed to concentrate on the bigger opportunities). Searching for the most efficient and lucrative strategies, it's no surprise where I turned...

An extreme surge in volatility volume in the market causes chaos; many of the trading bots lose their edge or get turned off altogether, institutions are forced to dump huge orders on the market, and the pipes that hold the market together start to crack and leak. These are the ideal conditions to cash in on glitch strategies!

March 2020 provided incredibly fertile hunting conditions. Unfortunately, there wasn't a glitch strategy unearthed that was quite as golden as that auction strategy that the Texas guys cashed in on in 2008, but it had the feel of the good old days (that's the "good old days" when the world's financial system was on the brink of collapse). It actually felt like I was trading back in 2001 when I collected that first paycheck trading my $MMM lagging strategy. Almost twenty years later, I was back doing the same thing, trading the $VXX when it lagged $SPY (they had an inverse relationship) and then quickly moving on to trading gold stocks that lagged the price of gold. It was good to be back playing my old game, and there was obviously plenty of edge in this strategy because this old-school gamer, now even slower on the keyboard, was making plenty of cash.

Another amazing glitch strategy—the one that revolves around the opening and closing auctions—was resurrected by the insane volatility. This had always been one of John's favorite strategies, and miraculously, the half-heartedness of his job search had paid off. He was still there in the office, with his head barely above water when the panic hit, and was able to take advantage of the craziness, refill his trading coffers and resurrect his own career. Mike also joined in, dropping his burgeoning poker career and jumping back into trading. We had to be quick to catch the truly insane volatility because once the markets realized that the world wasn't ending, volatility receded from its historic levels.

Volatility wasn't the only thing teetering out; my relationship quickly hit the rocks after I moved in with my new girlfriend. This came as no surprise, considering the markets and trading completely consumed me during my brief stay. I was more of a trading zombie than a charming boyfriend. I didn't want to make the same mistakes as in 2008, so my days were spent glued to my desk, only separated from my screens by one or two quick sprints to the toilet. When the market closed, my time was spent devouring the latest news on Twitter. I barely slept, and when I did sleep, I had the unpleasant dreams of Level 2 order books dancing in my head. I can be a bastard in the best of times, but unsurprisingly, I was especially unpleasant to be around during this frantic time.

Consequently, I got the boot from the apartment, and our relationship less than two weeks after I moved in. Cupid must have wept, but I hoped the trading gods appreciated my sacrifice. I returned to my apartment (which thankfully had gotten its internet connection upgraded) with a mild heartbreak and a mind and body exhausted from all the screen time. I had traded more shares in fourteen days than I had in almost the past year! I was a decrepit creature, having barely seen sunlight or walked a few hundred yards in the last two weeks. Despite my condition, and the fact that the panic had died down, it was no time to slam on the brakes; the trading gods were indeed being merciful.

I turned my attention to the cruise line sector for the rest of 2020. This sector was of course getting hit hard by COVID, so this sector had plenty of wild action. Not only were there big moves in this group, but the group's stocks followed each other nicely, making it a prime target for my lagging strategy. I would have the order books and charts for all the big companies in the sector scattered across my trading monitor, and look for any laggards when there were moves in the sector. The added bonus with this strategy is that I could read the tape on these stocks and try to buy before big buyers and sell before big sellers, and on top of that, the sector sometimes lagged the broad market, giving me yet another tell.

Out of the blue, 2020 turned out to be the most profitable year of my career. I was thanking my lucky stars while the rest of the world suffered through the pandemic. It wasn't much fun being holed up in my apartment for a year, devoid of human contact, apart from the occasional visit from my daughters, but I was well aware that my hardships were nothing compared to the pain and suffering going on elsewhere.

As 2021 began, panic had been vanquished from the markets and replaced with a sense of euphoria. During the heart of the pandemic, the central banks had pumped the world's economy full of cash, and a massive chunk of that cash had made its way to the U.S equity market. It flowed from the big financial institutions and from millions of amateur day traders, armed with pandemic handout checks, who were looking for a little excitement while locked away in their homes. This trading boom was like no other I'd seen before; every opportunist was opening a Robin Hood trading account and buying the latest meme stock pumped up by the message boards. This boom brought us countless 1000% moves in worthless speculative stocks and helped bring about an astronomical 30% bounce in the markets from the pandemic lows till the end of 2020.

Typically, when the market is strong, volatility drops and trading results suffer, but this time things were different. The markets were so wild, and the moves so ferocious, that the first half of 2021 turned out to be some of the best trading I had ever seen. What most traders will remember most about these insane times was the craziness of the Gamestop short squeeze. In a bid to say a big "Fuck you!" to Wall Street and, more importantly, make a ton of cash, a group of trading renegades hatched a cunning plan in a Reddit subgroup called Wallstreetbets. Their plan was a stunning success when they caused the Gamestop stock to make a 3000% move in just a few days! It was one of the wildest things I have ever seen in the markets.

After initially believing I was a little above scouring Reddit message boards for hot stock tips—which was a bit rich considering a YouTube video had saved my ass a couple of years prior—I swallowed my pride and joined the fray. I wasn't lucky or brave enough to catch the Gamestop move, but I made some cash in a similar message board-driven pump. During the height of the euphoria, I spent a weekend scouring the message boards, searching for this group's next target. It seemed this motley group was getting even more brazen after their recent successes and now was targeting silver, hoping to corner the market and cause a massive spike in the precious metal's price.

It was one thing to move the price of an antiquated retail company, but to move the price of a metal that everyone in the world was familiar with seemed like quite a challenge. Regardless, I got sucked into the hype and knew if the price of silver went up, then the stocks of silver miners would also go up. I hatched a plan. Once the pre-market session opened on Monday at 4 am New York time, while the legions of devoted Wallstreetbets followers were still sleeping, I would load up on my favorite silver mining stocks and beat all these suckers to the punch.

It worked to a tee. As soon as I loaded in, the two stocks I bought slowly crept up. As more "traders" rolled out of their beds in the U.S and jumped on their computers to buy silver and other related stocks, the higher my profits went. I held my positions for a few hours, then sold them to these fools who were late to the party. It ended up being my best trade ever! However, the second part of my plan wasn't so lucky. The physical bars of silver I panic-bought still sit collecting dust in an attic since these misfits failed to corner the silver markets.

The markets showed no sign of slowing, so I looked for the next spot to take advantage of this exuberance. It didn't take me long to find my next target: a sector of stocks called SPACs, or Special Acquisition Companies. I will call them sketchy IPOs, and they were all the craze in early 2021. They have a peculiar structure where they are redeemable at $10, so the strategy that I adopted–along with nearly every other savvy equity trader I knew–involved buying these stocks as close to $10 as possible, knowing that $10 was the downside, and then hoping for a nice spike up. Some of the spikes were gigantic; many of these SPACs were hit $20, $50, or even $100!

I don't know if this strategy qualifies as a glitch, but it definitely was a niche play with plenty of edge. Playing these SPACs meant deviating from scalping and holding my positions for days, weeks, or months. Considering the amazing risk/reward, it was well worth venturing out of my comfort zone. The most famous SPAC was the one that partnered with Donald Trump, $DWAC was the symbol. I remember vividly when the news of this partnership hit because I was in Amsterdam on holiday. The stock proceeded to move from $10 to $180 in the next two days and provide a massive payday for the legions of SPAC traders. Unfortunately, I wasn't so fortunate, and it wasn't because I boycotted the trade because of some political belief (I had gotten over that kind of thing years ago). It was because I attempted to take advantage of this momentous "trading event" on my laptop while sitting on the floor of the Van Gogh Museum after the receptors in my brain had been trumped by a mid-morning visit to a local coffee shop.

A trader always wants more, but despite some missed opportunities, I can't complain about my results in 2020 and 2021. I had my two best years as a trader, so a nice "V-bottomed bounce" pattern had developed in my fortunes since my capitulated state of a few years earlier.

I finally had a sturdy safety net for the first time in almost fifteen years, and although I still didn't have a yacht, I managed to buy an apartment in Spain, which was a better long-term investment in my own happiness than letting the money sit in a bank account or throwing it away on whims.

While at my apartment in late-February 2022, our "hero" volatility showed up again. This time, it was the Russian invasion of Ukraine that sparked panic in the markets—although it was a short-lived moment of opportunity for us traders, as markets have historically been quite fond of wars. However, returning to Poland, I saw real terror on the faces of the Ukrainian women and children who flooded the country as they fled the war. It was a stark reminder that behind every one of those spikes on a soulless chart on a computer when volatility occurs, there are real human beings who are suffering. It was a humbling experience and one that reinforced what I had come to appreciate during COVID—that many of my troubles of the last two decades as a trader have been self-made and are trivial compared to the suffering that others endure.

In fact, my struggles seem to be in the rearview mirror now; after 21 long years in the business, I am living the trader lifestyle that I dreamed of when I decided as a young man fresh out of college that I wanted to dedicate my life to this thing. I have a good life in Poland with my amazing daughters; regular trips to Spain, Texas, England, and other corners of the world; and have gained the confidence to make a prosperous living in my beloved profession even in rougher times. Of course, I've tasted success before, but as a young trader, it was hard to imagine that I could ever lose it all twice over and have to endure tough times. I thought it would all be gravy. Nowadays, I can appreciate the good times so much more, because I've seen the other side.

If you are thinking about this profession or already on your journey, I can't give you a golden ticket to riches, or even tell you exactly where you'll find glitches, but the stories I have shared can help give you an edge. I am not suggesting you follow my lead, instead learn from my mistakes. If I could leave you with one piece of advice, it would be to enjoy the good times, but remember that they can't last forever. Just like the markets, life has swings up and down, as well as periods of volatility that can cause you to panic. Ride the momentum through the good times, knowing that troubles will one day come again. And hang on in there during the bad times, because eventually every situation reaches a bottom from which the only way is up.

Acknowledgements

I would like to thank Tim Clayton, not only for all his invaluable help with this book but also for helping me discover the joy of writing.

Although I have many times regretted helping my little brother get into this brutal business, we are both somehow still standing after over 20 years. It's quite an accomplishment and it's been quite a ride. I wouldn't have been able to survive without John being there for me during the rough times, he is the best brother I could ask for.

Further Reading/Useful Resources

- https://www.david-hale.com/

- **Follow me on Twitter at:**
  https://twitter.com/CREAMtrader

- **Essex Oil Trader's $700m Glitch**
  https://www.ft.com/content/304b03cc-f5fa-4c36-b60b-5641cb199ef9

- **Facebook IPO Debacle Article Featuring John Hale Interview**
  https://www.wsj.com/articles/SB10001424052702304791704577416470248061722?mod=article_inline

- **ICO YouTube Instructional Video**
  https://www.youtube.com/watch?v=Y5i4IkkYMWw

Recommended Books

Reminiscences of a Stock Operator, Edwin Lefèvre (1923)

Flash Crash, Liam Vaughn (2020)

Dark Pools, Scott Patterson (2013)

Alpha trader, Brent Donnelly (2021)

Trading in the Zone, Mark Douglas (2001)

Zero to Hero, Yvan Byeajee (2015)

The Essence of Trading Psychology, Yvan Byeajee (2016)

Printed in Great Britain
by Amazon